Cassell's BEC Series – N

Accounting for Management:
Quantitative and Accounting Methods

Robert E. Counsell
B.A., F.C.A., A.C.M.A., A.T.I.I.

*Senior Lecturer,
Department of Commerce,
Bridgend College of Technology*

CASSELL · LONDON

CASSELL LTD
35 Red Lion Square, London WC1R 4SG
and at Sydney, Auckland, Toronto, Johannesburg,

an affiliate of Macmillan Publishing Co. Inc., New York

© R.E. Counsell 1980

All rights reserved. No part of this publication may be
reproduced, stored in a retrieval system, or transmitted, in
any form or by any means, electronic, mechanical,
photocopying, recording or otherwise, without the prior
permission in writing of the Publishers.

First published 1980

Typeset by Colset Private Limited, Singapore.

ISBN 0 304 30336 4

Printed in Great Britain by
Richard Clay (The Chaucer Press) Ltd,
Bungay, Suffolk

Contents

1 Introduction   1

I. Some Aspects of Costing

2 The Accounts of a Manufacturing Organisation   5
3 Stock Records   20
4 Overheads and their Recovery   28
5 Job Costing   32
6 Process Costing   40
7 Marginal Costing   48
8 Standard Costing   56

II. Forecasts and Budgets

9 Sampling and Forecasting Techniques   65
10 Budgetary Control: Its Uses and Limitations   85
11 The Preparation of Budgets   91

III. Analysis and Interpretation of Accounting Information

12 Capital   109
13 Cash Flow and Flow of Funds   120
14 Profitability   132
15 Ratio Analysis   142
16 Presentation of Information   157

IV. Inflation Accounting

17 Indices   175
18 Adjusting for Inflation   185

19 Additional Assignments   204

Answers to Numerical Questions   216

I. Introduction

Previous studies have been concerned with the picture that a business presents to the outside world; the results of the various purchases and sales of goods and services from which a profit or loss has resulted, as revealed in the trading and profit and loss accounts for an accounting period; and the overall position of the business at the end of that period — the assets that it owns, and the liabilities that it owes, as revealed by the balance sheet.

It is now proposed to look at the internal workings of a business — the many factors that must be taken into consideration before the transactions can take place that result in the financial accounts. Every business is run, or managed, either by the owner(s) or employees known as managers. People who run a business are required to make decisions, and sound decisions can only be made upon sound and accurate information. The supply of this information is the function of the accounting department. The information is called management information or management accounting. It is largely concerned with the cost of products, or the costs of running the several departments of a business, an aspect also known as cost accounting.

It is most important to remember that the function of an accountant — whether financial or management — is to communicate information, in the same way that an author does with the written word, and a speaker with the spoken word. The accountant is more fortunate. He may also use figures to back up his written words. The presentation of these figures is of vital importance. Correct communication to the reader is essential. A mere jumble of figures, even if they are correct, is useless unless the reader understands from them exactly what the accountant intends. Thought should, therefore, be given to meaningful presentation of all information.

Managers are busy people, and few are trained accountants. Too much detail confuses. The presentation of information should be as simple as possible, and easily understood by the audience for which it is intended. Information that is difficult to understand is usually ignored — and the accountant has only wasted his own and other people's valuable time.

Previous accountancy studies have been largely concerned with the type of business that trades. It buys finished goods from a variety of manufacturers, and sells them to its own customers at a price sufficiently high to cover the cost of the goods, the running expenses of the business, and then leave a margin of net profit for the trader. In this volume, the main concern will be with the manufacturing type of business — the one that manufactures the finished product that it then proceeds to sell to its customers. The techniques employed, however, may equally well be applied to a trading business, with a resultant improvement in efficiency.

Many of the problems used in this volume will be similar to those that are faced by people working in manufacturing industry. In attempting to solve the problems use will be made of several quantitative techniques. Once the domain of the statistician, they are now being used increasingly as effective accounting and management tools.

This study falls into four main sections:

I. Some basic aspects of costing techniques.
II. The techniques and methods used in forecasting and budgeting.
III. The analysis and interpretation of accounting information.
IV. The effect of inflation upon business results.

Part I
Some Aspects of Costing

2. The Accounts of a Manufacturing Organisation

The preparation of manufacturing accounts is a convenient point to switch from the study of financial to management accounting, with its predominantly costing background.

Financial accounts have been concerned with the preparation of a financial statement of the overall position of a business. A manufacturing account is similarly concerned with the overall situation, this time breaking the information down into greater detail, to show the several aspects of the organisation — the manufacturing side, the trading, and the overhead cost of running the business. The financial accountant is mainly concerned with grouping together all items of sales and expenditure that are of a like nature. The resulting information is then arranged to show how much gross profit has arisen from trading; how much the expenses of running the organisation have been; finally how much net profit has resulted from the activities of the period. The management accountant is more concerned with analysing the information between the various departments, and ultimately the products that are produced.

The manufacturing account represents a stage midway between these two concepts. It recognises two main categories of cost:
    (a)   Direct costs.
    (b)   Indirect costs, or overheads.

(a) Direct Costs

A direct cost is one that varies directly with production. If one extra unit of production is manufactured, there will be a specific amount of additional cost. If one less unit is produced, there will be a saving of this same amount of cost.

The direct costs are three in number.

(i) Direct (or Raw) Materials

Every item manufactured must have a direct material cost. It will comprise the cost of all materials used in the product, of sufficient value to be recorded specifically as being used. Take the example of a press shop, which presses small parts out of strips of metal. The metal used will be a major item of cost, and classified as direct materials. It will be recorded separately. If the pressed parts are then passed through a plating plant, to be given a protective coating of shiny metal, the minute amount of plating materials used will not be recorded separately. It will be treated as an indirect cost, and included in overheads.

Unless there is a fairly sophisticated costing system, it is often difficult to arrive at the cost of direct materials used. The figure is, therefore, calculated in a manner similar to the cost of sales in a trading account. To the opening stock of raw materials is added purchases for the period — after deducting returns — and also carriage inwards. The closing stock is deducted to give the cost of direct materials used. The format is as follows:

	£	£
Opening stock of raw materials		15 000
Add Purchases	105 000	
Less Returns	2 000	
	103 000	
Add Carriage inwards	2 500	105 500
		120 500
Less Closing stock of raw materials		20 000
Raw materials consumed		£100 500

(ii) Direct Labour

Manufacturing consists of acquiring materials and hiring labour to convert the materials into a product for sale. The labour that is used actually to alter the form of the materials is known as direct labour. More of this type of labour will be employed as production rises, and less as it falls. It is possible to calculate the exact direct labour cost of manufacturing one extra article of production. It is by this amount that direct labour cost will rise for each additional item produced.

It is important to categories labour accurately. In the manufacture of a book-case consisting of wooden shelves and sliding glass panels, direct labour will be concerned with cutting the wood to size; planing and smoothing it; shaping the corners; slotting to receive the glass panels; assembling; cutting the glass panels to size; smoothing the edges; cutting the handle slots; and finally staining and polishing the wood. Labour involved in storing the wood and glass, moving the materials to the shop floor and between productions processes, or the supervision and management of the labour force, does not in any way alter the workpiece. It cannot, therefore, be treated as direct labour.

(iii) *Direct Expenses*

These are few in number, but will all vary directly with the number of units produced. The best example is royalties. Where a product is manufactured under licence, a royalty must be paid to the owner of the patent, for each unit produced.

Do not confuse this with indirect items of expense. Electrical power, used for operating machines, will vary with production. The larger the number of units produced, the longer the machines will operate, and the greater will be the power consumed. The reverse occurs when production falls. Power usage, although varying generally in line with production, will not vary exactly. Other factors intervene, such as leaving machinery running during halts in production. As there is no direct variation with production, electrical power cannot be included under direct expense.

(iv) *Prime Cost*

The above three direct cost elements are added together to give the prime cost, or the total direct cost of production. This is an important sub-total, and should be shown on all statements of manufacturing cost.

	£
Direct materials	100 500
Direct labour	35 300
Direct expenses — Royalties	3 200
Prime cost	£139 000

(b) Indirect Costs or Overheads

The only overheads included in the manufacturing account are:

Works Overheads

These comprise all the other expenses involved in running a factory, other than the direct or prime cost of the product. These include;

Indirect labour	The wages of storemen, fork-lift truck drivers, labourers and cleaners.
Management and supervisory labour	Works and production managers, superintendents, foremen and chargehands.
Factory light, heat and power	Electricity, gas, oil and coal.
Depreciation	Works machinery only.
Factory rent and rates	
Canteen expenses	
Consumables	Small items of material not sufficiently large to merit the cost and effort of allocating as direct materials e.g. greases, wipers, coolant, small nuts and bolts etc.
Repairs and renewals	Machinery and factory buildings, including the cost of the maintenance section.

These works overheads are grouped together and sub-totalled, then added to the prime cost.

	£	£
Prime cost		139 000
Works overheads:		
Indirect labour	40 000	
Depeciation of machinery	15 000	
Factory rent and rates	12 000	
Consumables	8 000	
Repairs to machinery	11 000	
Repairs to buildings	3 000	89 000
		£228 000

Work in Progress Stock

Accounts, whether annual or monthly, are presented for a period which ends on a specific date. On this date there will always be some items of production that have been started, but not yet finished. Some will barely have been started, while others will be almost complete. All will be evaluated, and included under the work in progress heading.

In the manufacturing account the cumulative cost to date will be adjusted by adding to it the work in progress stock at the beginning of the period, and deducting that at the end. The evaluation of the stock includes prime cost and works overheads.

The resulting figure represents the cost of goods produced during the period, and is transferred to the trading account.

	£
Cost to date	228 000
Add Opening stock of work in progress	6 000
	234 000
Less Closing stock of work in progress	5 000
Cost of finished goods produced	£229 000

It is important to note that a manufacturing account is a statement of the cumulative build-up of the cost of producing the products of a business.

Trading Account

The object of a trading account is to calculate the cost of goods sold, take this away from the sales value of those goods, and finally reveal the gross or trading profit. It is constructed as for a trading organisation, with the cost of finished goods replacing normal purchases. If there are any goods purchased for resale — where, for example, a firm offers to its customers a wider range of products than it produces — they will be included in the trading account next to the goods produced. The figures are adjusted for the opening and closing stocks of finished goods.

	£	£
Sales		360 000
Opening stock of finished goods	20 000	
Add Cost of goods produced	229 000	
Goods for resale	20 000	
	269 000	
Less Closing stock of finished goods	24 000	
Cost of sales	245 000	
Gross profit	115 000	
	£360 000	£360 000

Profit and Loss Account

The object of the profit and loss account is to collect the costs of running the business, deduct them from the gross profit, to leave the net profit for the accounting period.

In preparing the simple profit and loss account of a trading organisation, the order of presenting overheads is not important. The management of a manufacturing organisation prefers to have the expenses analysed under three principal headings, each representing a function of management:

(i) Administration overheads.
(ii) Selling and distribution overheads.
(iii) Financial overheads.

(i) Administration Overheads

This covers the expense of administering the organisation, and includes items such as:

Salaries	For the following functions — secretarial, accounting, buying and personnel.
Depreciation	Of office equipment.
Light and heat	Of offices.
Rent and rates	Of offices.
Printing and stationery	
Telephone and postages	
Audit fee	For the annual review of the financial results by an independent accountant in public practice.
Legal fees	

(ii) Selling and Distribution Overheads

This includes all the costs of selling and distributing the product, such as:

Salespersons' salaries and commission.
Agents' commission.
Advertising.
Entertaining and travelling.
Motor expenses.
Depreciation of motor vehicles.
Commercial vehicle expenses.
Carriage outwards – the cost of hiring the services of outside haulage contractors to deliver goods to customers.
Despatch Department costs will also fall under this heading, unless responsibility rests with the works manager, when it will form a works overhead.

(iii) Financial Overheads

Here are allocated the costs of raising finance for the organisation. They include:

Bank charges.
Loan interest.
Discounts allowed.

Any payment to the owners as interest or dividend on capital introduced into the business will not be included.

The profit and loss account will appear like this:

	£	£	£
Gross profit			115 000
Administration overheads:			
Salaries	25 000		
Depreciation – Office equipment	1 000		
Light and heat of offices	3 000		
Rent and rates of offices	5 000		
Telephone, postages and stationery	6 000	40 000	
Selling and distribution overheads:			
Salaries and commission – Salespersons	18 000		
Agents' commission	3 000		
Advertising	4 000		
Motor expenses	3 000		
Depreciation – Motor vehicles	2 000		
Carriage outwards	5 000	35 000	
Financial overheads:			
Bank charges and interest	1 000		
Loan interest	3 000		
Discounts allowed	1 000	5 000	
Net profit		35 000	
		£115 000	£115 000

A complete worked example will appear as follows.

The following balances have been extracted from the books of Softoys, a local toy manufacturer, at 30th May 19-7.

The Accounts of a Manufacturing Organisation 13

	£
Stock of raw materials, 1st June 19-6	5 000
Stock of work in progress, 1st June 19-6	2 000
Stock of finished goods, 1st June 19-6	1 500
Direct wages	24 000
Indirect factory wages	7 000
Royalties	1 100
Purchases of raw materials	53 000
Plant and machinery	25 000
Office equipment	8 000
Factory power	5 000
Factory consumables	4 000
Factory rent and rates	6 000
Carriage inwards	1 300
Carriage outwards	3 500
Administration salaries	8 000
Salespersons' salaries	10 000
Commission on sales	4 000
Salespersons' motor expenses	4 000
Telephone	2 400
Stationery	2 800
Bank charges	1 400
Loan interest	700
Discounts allowed	660
Goods for resale	8 400
Returns inwards	800
Returns outwards	300
Sales	165 000

The following information is also available:

(1) Stocks at 31st May 19-7   – Raw materials   £4 000
                                       – Work in progress   £2 500
                                       – Finished goods   £2 800
(2) Depreciate machinery at 10% per annum, and office equipment at 15% per annum.
(3) Production wages due, but not yet paid, £740.
(4) A bad debt amounting to £300 is to be written off.

REQUIRED: Prepare a Manufacturing, Trading and Profit and Loss Account for the year to 31st May 19-7.

Softoys
Manufacturing, Trading and Profit and Loss Account for the year to 31st May 19-7

	£	£	£
Opening stock of raw materials		5 000	
Add Purchases of raw materials	53 000		
Less Returns outwards	300		
	52 700		
Add Carriage inwards	1 300	54 000	
		59 000	
Less Closing stock of raw materials		4 000	
Raw materials consumed		55 000	
Direct wages		24 740	
Royalties		1 100	
Prime cost		80 840	
Works overheads:			
Indirect factory wages	7 000		
Factory power	5 000		
Factory consumables	4 000		
Factory rent and rates	6 000		
Depreciation – machinery	2 500	24 500	
		105 340	
Add Opening stock of work in progress		2 000	
		107 340	
Less Closing stock of work in progress		2 500	
		104 840	
Cost of goods produced carried to Trading Account			104 840
		£104 840	£104 840
Sales (net of returns)			164 200
Opening stock of finished goods		1 500	
Add Goods produced		104 840	

	£	£	£
Goods for resale		8 400	
		114 740	
Less Closing stock finished goods		2 800	
		111 940	
Gross profit c/d		52 260	
		£164 200	£164 200
Gross profit b/d			52 260
Administration overheads:			
Salaries	8 000		
Telephones	2 400		
Stationery	2 800		
Depreciation – office equipment	1 200	14 400	
Selling and distribution overheads:			
Salespersons' salaries	10 000		
Commission on sales	4 000		
Motor expenses	4 000		
Carriage outwards	3 500	21 500	
Financial overheads:			
Bank charges	1 400		
Loan interest	700		
Discounts allowed	660	2 760	
Net profit for the year		13 600	
		£52 260	£52 260

Market Value of Manufactured Goods

The above format merely informs us that the business has made a gross profit of £52 260. This has arisen from the efforts of the works team in producing the goods, and the sales team in selling them. It is not known how much profit has arisen from each team's efforts.

To overcome this, it is possible to value the finished goods transferred to the trading account at the market value they would have cost to purchase. This will separate the manufacturing profit from the sales profit. Both will then be carried to the profit and loss account.

The summarised figures for Softoys would then appear as follows:

Manufacturing, Trading and Profit and Loss Account for the year to 31st. May 19 – 7

	£	£
(Debits as before)		
Production cost of goods completed	104 840	
Market value of goods produced carried to trading account		127 000
Gross profit on manufacturing carried to Profit and Loss Account	22 160	
	£127 000	£127 000
Sales (net of returns)		164 200
Opening stock of finished goods	1 500	
Add Market value of goods produced	127 000	
Goods for resale	8 400	
	136 900	
Less Closing stock of finished goods	2 800	
	134 100	
Gross profit on trading	30 100	
	£164 200	£164 200
Gross profit on manufacturing		22 160
Gross profit on trading		30 100
		£52 260

Assignments

2.1. Into which nominal ledger accounts will the following transactions be posted?
   (a) Wages paid to a fork lift truck driver.
   (b) Rates for the factory area.
   (c) Purchase of envelopes.

The Accounts of a Manufacturing Organisation

(d) Hire of the services of a transport contractor, to collect a delivery of raw materials from a supplier.
(e) Bank charges.
(f) Petrol used in a salesperson's car.
(g) Repairs to a lathe used in the main production shop.
(h) Depreciation of an accounting machine.
(j) Oil used for works heating.
(k) Advertising a product in a trade journal.
(l) A major component used in a product.
(m) Salary of the production manager.
(n) Debt collection costs.
(p) Hotel bills for a sales conference.
(q) Interest on loan stock.

2.2. From the following information calculate:
(a) Prime cost.
(b) Total production cost.

	£
Canteen expenses (75% works)	20 000
Depreciation of machinery	31 000
Indirect labour	57 000
Raw materials	214 000
Opening stock of work in progress	19 000
Consumables	17 000
Productive wages	88 000
Repairs to machinery	19 000
Repairs to buildings (30% office)	10 000
Royalties	7 000
Rent and Rates (15% office)	20 000
Closing stock of work in progress	21 000

2.3. The following balances have been extracted from the books of the Tanguy Patent Milking Machine Company at 30th June 19-7:

	£
Repairs to plant	3 500
Stock of work in progress 1st July 19-6	2 400
Direct labour	9 700
Goods for resale	10 000
Office rent and rates	1 000

	£
Motor expenses for salespersons' cars	800
Purchases of raw material	24 000
Depreciation of plant	2 000
Salespersons' salaries	2 500
Stationery	400
Carriage inwards	1 200
Loan interest	900
Factory power, heat and light	5 000
Raw material stock, 1st July 19-6	1 000
Administration salaries	4 000
Discounts allowed	300
Salespersons' entertainment and travelling	400
Office light and heat	1 000
Rent and rates of works	4 100
Carriage outwards	1 200
Works indirect labour	4 000
Telephone and postages	300
Bank charges	800
Stock finished goods, 1st July 19-6	3 000
Salespersons' commission	1 000
Sales	81 000

Notes
(1) Closing stocks at 30th June 19-7
    Materials   £1 500
    Work in progess   £2 600
    Finished goods   £3 500
(2) Accruals for direct wages   – £300
(3) Prepayment of works rent   – £100

REQUIRED: Prepare a Manufacturing, Trading and Profit and Loss Account from the above information for the year to 30th June 19-7.

2.4. Richard P. Green is a master baker. On 30th June 19-8 the following balances were extracted from his books of account.

	£
Repairs to plant	3 200
Direct wages	10 200
Motor expenses	1 100

	£
Depreciation of plant	1 800
Stationery	350
Loan Interest	900
Opening stock of raw materials	4 500
Office rent and rates	950
Purchases	29 000
Salespersons' salaries	4 000
Opening stock work in progress	4 000
Carriage outwards	1 700
Salaries of office staff	3 000
Entertainment and travelling	390
Rent and rates of works	5 220
Telephone and postages	410
Sales	90 000
Power and heat of works	7 000
Discount allowed	250
Heat and light of office	840
Works indirect labour	4 720
Carriage inwards	740
Opening stock of finished goods	1 100
Bank charges	650
Commission paid to agents	840

You are given the following information:

(1) Closing stocks – Raw materials £4 100
Work in progress £4 860
Finished goods £ 700
(2) Direct wages due, but not yet paid £ 300
(3) Factory rental paid in advance £ 120
(4) The market value of production was calculated to be £70 000.

REQUIRED: Prepare a Manufacturing, Trading and Profit and Loss Account for the year to 30th June 19-8, showing the profit derived from manufacturing and trading functions separately.

3. Stock Records

The simplest form of trading activity consists of finding a buyer for goods, and then purchasing those goods for delivery to the customer. Purchases are only made when a customer has been found. Some delay is inevitable, and customers usually demand a prompt service. The problem is overcome by holding a supply of goods, known as stock, from which customers are supplied with very little delay. In the case of a manufacturing business, stock-holding is inevitable. The organisation is more complex than for a pure trading operation. Direct workers are supplied with raw materials and the use of machinery, in order to make products. If raw materials are not available when required, the work force stands idle. This adversely affects the profitability of the business.

In a small business, stock is easily ascertained by a visual inspection of the stores. In a larger business it is necessary to have written records of stock and stock movements. If the records are properly designed and maintained, they can give much valuable information. The quantity and value of stock in hand at any time can be easily seen. Advance warning of shortages can be given, with the consequent need to re-order stock.

Stock represents value which must be paid for in cash. This concept is often not appreciated, yet stock ties up the cash resources of a business just as effectively as placing bundles of £5 notes on the shelves. No one would ever consider placing piles of notes on the shop floor, and then driving a fork lift truck over them. Not so with stock. Unless there is strict control excessive quantities of stock will be placed on the floor, and damaged through carelessness. A passing truck may accidentally tear the corner of a sack of plastic granules. In a very short time the contents of the sack will have spilled over the floor, been contaminated with grease and dirt, and be useless for production purposes.

It is normal to house stock in bonded stores, under the control of a storeman, with no access for unauthorised persons. There it can be kept safely, and issued only in the quantities required for production, and when properly authorised. Issues to production must be in strict rotation, using the oldest stock first. Much stock deteriorates with age, and may become useless for production purposes. The quantity of stock must also be kept within limits. It must not be so high that it ties up excessive amounts of capital. On the other hand, it must never be allowed to run so low that production is adversely affected by material shortages. For these reasons the keeping of effective stores records is a necessity for all but the smallest of businesses.

There are three principal methods of recording stock, each of which gives rise to a different valuation. These are:

(*a*) First In, First Out (FIFO)
(*b*) Last In, First Out (LIFO)
(*c*) Average Cost (AvCo)

The effect of the different methods can be seen by taking the following information and processing it by the above three methods. It must be emphasised that these are methods of recording stock values only. In practice, regardless of the method used, stores issues will always be made in strict rotation, so that stock has no chance to deteriorate through age.

The following details relate to ¼ h.p. electric motors for the year 19-0.

January	Received 100 units @ £4.00	= £400
March	Issued 60 units	
June	Received 70 units @ £4.20	= £294
September	Issued 50 units	
November	Received 60 units @ £4.50	= £270
December	Issued 80 units	

(a) First In, First Out

This method assumes that the first goods to be issued are the ones that have been longest in stock. The result is that stock is always valued at the up-to-date cost of buying materials.

Date 19-0	Received and price	Issued and price	Stock and value
January	100 @ £4.00 = £400		100@£4.00 = £400
March		60 @ £4.00 = £240	40@£4.00 = £160
June	70 @ £4.20 = £294		40@£4.00 = £160 70@£4.20 = £294 _____ £454
September		40 @ £4.00 = £160 10 @ £4.20 = £ 42 _____ £202	60@£4.20 = £252
November	60 @ £4.50 = £270		60@£4.20 = £252 60@£4.50 = £270 _____ £522
December		60 @ £4.20 = £252 20 @ £4.50 = £ 90 _____ £342	40@£4.50 = £180

(b) Last In, First Out

With this method it is assumed that the latest goods received will be issued first. Closing stock is always valued at the cost of the oldest purchases. In a period of inflation this means that stock will always appear to be undervalued, but issues to production will always be at the latest price. By raising the cost of the final article, this forces the business to keep selling prices under constant review. Application for price increases can then be made as early as possible, thereby offsetting the increase in costs.

Date 19-0	Received and price	Issued and price	Stock and value
January	100 @ £4.00 = £400		100@£4.00 = £400
March		60 @ £4.00 = £240	40@£4.00 = £160
June	70 @ £4.20 = £294		40@£4.00 = £160 70@£4.20 = £294 _____ £454

Stock Records 23

Date 19-0	Received and price	Issued and price	Stock and value
September		50 @ £4.20 = £210	40@£4.00 = £160 20@£4.20 = £ 84 ———— £244
November	60 @ £4.50 = £270		40@£4.00 = £160 20@£4.20 = £ 84 60@£4.50 = £270 ———— £514
December		60 @ £4.50 = £270 20 @ £4.20 = £ 84 ———— £354	40@£4.00 = £160

(c) Average Cost

With this method stock is valued at the average cost of the goods in hand. The stock-holding value is only altered when goods are received. All future issues are then priced at that average holding price, until further goods are received. The method is a combination of LIFO and FIFO and gives a stock valuation which lies between the two. Less detailed records are required, but the holding unit cost must be calculated after each receipt of goods.

Date 19-0	Receipts	Issues	Average unit cost of stock held	Number of units of stock	Total stock value £
January	100 @ £4.00	—	£4.00	100	400
March	—	60	£4.00	40	160
June	70 @ £4.20	—	£4.13	110	454
September	—	50	£4.13	60	248
November	60 @ £4.50	—	£4.32	120	518
December	—	80	£4.32	40	173

24 Accounting for Management

The average cost of the stock is found by adding together the cost of the existing stock, and the cost of the newly acquired stock, and dividing by the number of stock units then held.

Often stock valuation is only required for the purposes of calculating stock to be used in financial accounts. In such cases it is possible to compute stock on a periodic basis. It is necessary to record only the quantities issued and received, and the unit costs of goods received. At the end of each period the stock is calculated without reference to the individual purchases of stock, or their issue.

(*a*) FIFO – Total issues are deducted from total receipts, and the balance remaining is valued at the latest purchase prices, consistent with the quantities in stock.

(*b*) LIFO – The quantities in stock will be valued at the earliest purchase price, the calculation again being done in total.

(*c*) AvCo – The overall average for the period is calculated, and all issues priced at that rate.

Under FIFO and LIFO the stock value will differ under periodic inventory compared to perpetual inventory, if the stock is greater than the last, or first, purchase of goods.

The effect of periodic inventory can be illustrated from the original example if accounts are to be prepared at the end of June and December, and stock values are required at each date.

(*a*) FIFO

			Units
(i) June 19-0	Total received		
	(100 @ £4.00 + 70 @ £4.20)		170
	Issues		60
	Stock		110
			£
	Stock Value:	40 @ £4.00	160
		+ 70 @ £4.20	294
			454
(ii) December 19-0	Total received		
	(Opening stock 40 @ £4.00		
	+ 70 @ £4.20		Units
	+ 60 @ £4.50)		170
	Issues	(50 + 80)	130
	Stock		40

			£
	Stock Value	40 @ £4.50	180

(b) *LIFO*

(i) *June 19-0*   Stock, calculated as above   110

		£
Stock value	100 @ £4.00	400
	10 @ £4.20	42
		442

(ii) *December 19-0*   Stock, calculated as above   40

		£
Stock Value	40 @ £4.00	160

(c) *AvCo*

In both the above illustrations, the end of year stock has been the same for periodic as for perpetual inventory methods. This can often happen. In the case of AvCo, this will rarely be the case.

(i) *June 19-0*   Stock, calculated as above   110

Average cost of 170 units, costing £694

$$= \frac{£694}{170} = £4.08$$

		£
Stock Value 110 @ £4.08		449

(ii) *December 19-0*   Stock, calculated as above   40

Average cost of 170 units, costing £719

$$= \frac{£719}{170} = £4.23$$

		£
Stock Value	40 @ £4.23	169

The main conclusion to be drawn from the above illustration is that stock evaluation cannot be exact. Values will vary according to

26 Accounting for Management

the method of calculation. There are advantages and disadvantages in all the systems. The accountancy profession is worried by these variations. In order to attempt to standardise stock calculations, statements of standard accounting practice have been issued. The latest thought is that LIFO and AvCo give a truer reflection of fact than any other. The one principle that must always be applied is consistency. Having once decided on a method, it should be strictly adhered to, and altered only after careful consideration.

Assignments

3.1. Why is a strong system of stock control vital to a business?

3.2. Why is it necessary to follow a consistent policy of stock recording and evaluation? Illustrate your answer with examples.

3.3. Record the following transactions in the stores ledger of a wholesaler, using the FIFO perpetual inventory basis.

January	Received 86 units at a total cost of £430
March	Issued 60 units
May	Issued 20 units
July	Received 80 units @ £5.10 each
September	Issued 72 units
November	Received 84 units at a total cost of £441
December	Issued 77 units

3.4. Record the above using the LIFO perpetual inventory method.

3.5. Recalculate using the AvCo perpetual inventory basis of valuation.

3.6. Recalculate using the periodic inventory basis, valuing stock at the end of June and December, using

   (a)   FIFO
   (b)   LIFO
   (c)   AvCo

3.7. The issues represent sales, which are made at £7.50 per unit up to 30th June, and at £8.00 per unit thereafter. Calculate the trading profit (gross profit) for each half year, using the perpetual inventory basis under

(a) FIFO
(b) LIFO
(c) AvCo

3.8. Calculate trading profits for the same periods as in 3.7, but using the periodic inventory basis in all cases.

4. Overheads and their Recovery

The costs of a business are of two types — direct and indirect. The direct costs vary directly with production. If one additional unit of production is made, there will be a measurable increase in direct cost. When one unit less is made, there will be similar measurable decrease in direct cost. Direct — or raw — material is normally the largest component of direct cost. It includes all items of material that are of sufficient size to warrant the effort of charging directly to the job. Small items, such as glue, paint and small quantities of nails, screws and rivets, do not merit the clerical effort involved in charging directly to the job, and would be recovered as an overhead.

Direct wages will vary directly with production where remuneration is based upon piecework only. This means that a specific amount is paid when a production operation is successfully finished. If it is not finished, no payment is made. In this book it is assumed that direct labour is of this nature. Many organisations remunerate labour on the basis of a large basic wage, topped up with a productivity bonus. The basic element is paid regardless of the level of production. In such cases wages will not vary directly with production, and fall into the category of an indirect cost or overhead.

Overhead is a general term applied to all the costs involved in running a business, other than direct costs. It covers the costs of running the works organisation; product research and development; the administration of the business; selling and distributing the product; and the cost of raising finance. Overheads are diverse, covering the whole of the business organisation. The management accountant has the problem of allocating these costs to the individual product lines being manufactured.

Cost Centres

To help in this task, the organisation is split up into cost centres. These are areas of activity to which are gathered all costs of a like nature. A maintenance department, canteen and stores are examples of cost centres. Normally centres will identify with physical areas of the organisation. A stores cost centre is a physical area in which materials are kept, while awaiting issue to production. A centre may also not be identifiable with a physical area. The finance cost centre will gather together all the costs of raising finance for the business, other than from owners or shareholders. It is a function of the administration department, and cannot be identified with a physical area of the business.

Where a cost centre has a product which is being manufactured, it is known as a product centre. Examples are a machine shop which is machining parts for assembly into the saleable product in an assembly shop. Where a centre has a product that is saleable, thus giving rise to an income, it is also known as a profit centre. It is capable of showing a profit or loss on its overall activities.

Cost Allocation

The management accountant's task is to allocate the many, diverse overheads, onto the cost of each product manufactured. It is a major task requiring the use of many different bases of allocation. The allocation of direct cost to a product can be precise. In the case of overhead allocation an element of logical guesstimation enters. There is a two-fold process, firstly to collect all overhead costs onto the product or profit centres; and secondly to load the overheads onto each product passing through the centre.

(a) Re-allocation to Product Centres

Having allocated all the overheads of the business to their appropriate cost centres, the accountant must next re-allocate them to the product centres. The method employed to achieve this will vary with each cost centre. Canteen costs can best be re-allocated on the basis of numbers of employees in the other centres. It would be wrong to base it upon the numbers using the canteen facility, as it is provided for the benefit of all employees, whether they use it or not. Maintenance department overheads are best allocated on the basis of the time spent in repairing equipment in each cost centre or product centre. For this purpose time record sheets should be kept by each maintenance employee. Spare parts used in the repairs will have been charged directly to the appropriate centre, and will not be included in the maintenance department overheads that are being re-allocated. Heating and lighting costs can be allocated on the basis of cubic capacity of each cost centre. Rent and rates can be allocated on the floor areas of each centre. Power — the cost of driving machinery — will be allocated on the basis of meter readings. Each overhead, or group of overheads will be dealt with separately. In all cases there should be a logical basis for the method of allocation, or re-allocation used.

(b) *Allocation to Product*

Having collected all overheads of the organisation onto the product centres, the accountant must next load them onto the individual products. Most overheads accrue on a time basis. Labour is paid for the time spent at work. Rent and rates are paid for the period of occupation of premises. Depreciation charges are allied to the period of use of fixed assets. The method used to load the overheads onto the products that are manufactured must also be closely related to the passage of time. This is best achieved by using for the basis either direct labour hours spent in producing the product, or alternatively the number of machine hours. Both methods require a record of time spent — or estimated to be spent — on production of each product. A simpler, frequently used method is a percentage based upon the direct labour content of the product. This is an inferior method, as varying wage rates can affect the end result, but it has the advantage of simplicity.

The subject will be dealt with in greater detail in Chapter 5.

Assignments

4.1. Why is it easier to allocate direct costs than overheads to products?

4.2. Distinguish between cost and product centres, giving examples of each.

4.3. Your company allocates overheads to products on the basis of sales value. The managing director has asked you to submit a report to the next board meeting, recommending a more logical basis of allocation. What are your recommendations?

4.4. You are the management accountant of a medium sized manufacturing company. Submit a report outlining a method of collection of overheads, and their re-allocation to products.

5. Job Costing

A business will structure its costing system to suit its own particular needs. If it is manufacturing a large product, which passes through several operations, it may adopt a system of job costing. If the product is manufactured in batches, each batch will form a separate job. This is called batch costing, and is a variation of job costing.

Each job will be given a number, and will collect its own costs as it passes through production centres. Raw materials will be issued from the stores and allocated to the job number. Only significant amounts of material will be charged in this way. The stores issue notes will be priced and extended and charged to the job cost. Materials bought specifically for the job will be charged directly to the job cost. Each direct worker will record the time spent on each job on a time sheet. From this his wages will be charged to each job cost. The recording of tasks of only a few minutes duration will be too burdensome, so operations of a quarter of an hour or more only will be recorded.

The recording of material and labour costs is a relatively simple task, but overheads provide a more difficult problem. (See Chapter 4.) The dual problem of re-allocating overheads to product cost centres, and finally allocating to the product, will now be considered in greater detail.

(a) Allocation of Overheads to Product Cost Centres

It is possible to allocate directly to a cost centre such overheads as relate specifically to it. Indirect labour, for example, can be allocated on the basis of the cost centres in which the employees work. Rent and rates can be allocated on the basis of floor area. Heating is best allocated on the basis of the cubic capacity of each cost centre. Depreciation can be charged on the basis of the actual cost of the fixed assets, and the depreciation rate used in each department. The split of the power charge can be based on the electrical rating of the machines used in each cost centre. A better method, which is not always available, is separate metering of the supply to each department. By such means overheads can be logically allocated to each department.

Some cost centres will be service centres, in that they will not be directly concerned with production. The overheads of these centres must be re-allocated to the production cost centres on as logical a basis as can be devised. Take a business having three production cost centres — machine shop, plating shop and fitting shop. The machine shop is where components are machined from lengths of metal bar or rod. In the plating shop, plate steel is cut to size, bent and welded together. The fitting shop is where the final product is assembled, bringing together machined components, welded fabrications, and parts specially purchased from outside suppliers. In addition there are cost centres for canteen and welfare, maintenance department, drawing office, and stores. A logical basis of allocation for each of these service centres must be found.

(1) *Canteen and Welfare* The canteen and welfare service is provided to meet the needs of all employees of the business. A logical basis of re-allocation for the costs will be the numbers of employees working in each centre. This applies not only to the product cost centres, but to the non-productive centres as well.

(2) *Maintenance Department* The best method of re-allocation of this centre is to base it upon the time actually spent in working at each cost centre. Materials used in repairing equipment will be charged directly to the relevant cost centre. Only the overheads of the department, including labour, will need to be apportioned. A simpler, but far less effective, method of re-allocation of the costs of this department is on the basis of machinery value in each of the product cost centres. As canteen overheads have already been re-allocated, there is no need to apportion maintenance charges to that cost centre. To do so will mean having to commence re-allocation of that cost centre once more.

34 *Accounting for Management*

(3) *Drawing Office*   This is the department that prepares engineering drawings of each product. These are then used by the production departments to guide them in the manufacture of each job. The time involved in the preparation of each drawing must be accurately logged to each of the production centres, and the drawing office costs re-allocated on that basis.

(4) *Stores*   Stores costs can be re-allocated in a variety of ways:
(*a*) Floor area allocated to the materials of each product centre. This becomes difficult where there are large stocks of material which are common to more than one product centre.
(*b*) Value of stores issued. The figure is obtained by evaluating stores requisition notes. This method can be misleading where one product centre takes materials that are high in value but small in bulk and weight, while another takes heavy and bulky materials of low value.
(*c*) The number of stores requisitions issued by each department. When a stores requisition is received in the stores, the storeman will follow a set pattern. He will go around the stores collecting the parts required, and deliver them to the person who has presented the requisition. At each bin will be a bin card recording the number of items in stock. This will be adjusted by the quantity issued. Finally the issued items will be recorded in a stores ledger. On the average each requisition will take a roughly similar period of time to process, and forms a logical basis for re-allocating the costs of the department. It will be inaccurate if one department's materials are easy to dispense, while those of another are difficult, similarly if one department issues single item requisitions, while another issues multi-item ones. Such occasions are rare.

Let us now work through an example of a business having the departments mentioned in the text above. The following information is available.

	Overheads	Employees	Maintenance time spent	Drw. Off. time spent	Stores requisitions
Machine Shop	£54 000	58	5 120 h	4 500 h	9 700
Plating Shop	£88 000	54	6 210 h	3 750 h	12 200
Fitting Shop	£72 000	40	5 610 h	3 700 h	9 300
Canteen	£17 000	3	—	—	—
Maintenance	£42 000	8	—	—	—
Drawing Office	£35 000	6	100 h	—	—
Stores	£15 000	4	80 h	—	—

The overhead costs will be allocated as follows:

(a) *Canteen*

	Employees	£
Machine Shop	58	5 800
Plating Shop	54	5 400
Fitting Shop	40	4 000
Maintenance	8	800
Drawing Office	6	600
Stores	4	400
	170	£17 000

(b) *Maintenance*

	Time spent (h)	£
Machine Shop	5 120	12 800
Plating Shop	6 210	15 525
Fitting Shop	5 610	14 025
Drawing Office	100	250
Stores	80	200
	17 120	£42 800

(c) *Drawing Office*

	Time spent (h)	£
Machine Shop	4 500	13 500
Plating Shop	3 750	11 250
Fitting Shop	3 700	11 100
	11 950	£35 850

(d) *Stores*

	Requisitions	£
Machine Shop	9 700	4 850
Plating Shop	12 200	6 100
Fitting Shop	9 300	4 650
	31 200	£15 600

In tabular form the allocations will be:

36 Accounting for Management

	Canteen £	Maintenance £	Drawing Office £	Stores £	Total £
	£	£	£	£	£	£
Machine Shop	54 000	5 800	12 800	13 500	4 850	90 950
Plating Shop	88 000	5 400	15 525	11 250	6 100	126 275
Fitting Shop	72 000	4 000	14 025	11 100	4 650	105 775
Canteen	17 000	(17 000)	—	—	—	—
Maintenance	42 000	800	(42 800)	—	—	—
Drawing Office	35 000	600	250	(35 850)	—	—
Stores	15 000	400	200	—	(15 600)	—
	£323 000	—	—	—	—	£323 000

The next problem is to allocate the overheads on each cost centre to the jobs that pass through them. The direct wages content of each job can be used to allocate overheads, but there will be a distortion. People performing the same job can be paid at different basic rates. Despite this, it is a simple method, and frequently used. A better method, which eliminates the distortion, is to allocate on a time basis. If the product centre has a predominance of hand labour, it is best to allocate overheads on the basis of direct labour hours worked on each job. If the product centre has many machines working, it is better to allocate on the basis of machine hours. In both cases the overhead recovery rate will be calculated by dividing total overheads by the total number of direct labour or machine hours worked during the period.

In the example it is assumed that the machine shop is predominantly machine labour, while the other two are hand labour. The machine and direct labour hours worked are:

Machine Shop	9 095 machine hours
Plating Shop	42 092 direct labour hours
Fitting Shop	42 310 direct labour hours

The overhead recovery rates will now be:

Machine Shop $\quad \dfrac{£90\,950}{9\,095} = £10$ per machine hour

Plating Shop $\quad \dfrac{£126\,275}{42\,092} = £3$ per direct labour hour

Fitting Shop $\quad \dfrac{£105\,775}{42\,310} = £2.50$ per direct labour hour

Using these overhead recovery rates, it is now possible to prepare a job cost.

Example

Product A is being manufactured for a customer. Calculate the job cost from the following information:

	Machine Shop	Plating Shop	Fitting Shop
Raw materials	£40	£120	£90
Hourly wage rate	£2.20	£2.00	£2.50
Direct labour hours	5	8	6
Machine hours	2	—	—

The cost will be:

	Machine Shop £	Plating Shop £	Fitting Shop £	Total £
Raw Materials	40	120	90	250
Direct labour	11	16	15	42
Overheads*	20	24	15	59
	£71	£160	£120	£351

* Recovered at rates given in text above.

Job Quotations

A job cost is an actual, historical cost, calculated at a future time when figures are available. If a potential customer requests a quotation for the supply of a job at a future date, actual figures obviously cannot be available. It is then necessary to estimate. This is done in the following way.

(a) *Raw Materials* The estimated usage on the job is multiplied by the estimated future cost of the material.

(b) *Direct Labour* The estimated time that will be taken to manufacture the job is multiplied by the estimated future wage rates.

(c) *Overheads* Future overheads and their basis of apportionment are budgeted, and divided by budgeted labour or machine hours. This gives the estimated overhead recovery rates.

The cost will then be prepared in a manner similar to that given above.

Assignments

5.1. Suction Products Ltd manufacture industrial pumps, usually to customers' specification. Job Z 1793 has just been completed, and you are required to prepare a job cost, to determine the profit or loss on the job. The job passes through four product centres, A, B, C and D. Overheads are recovered on the basis of direct labour hours in A and C, and on the basis of machine hours in B and D. The selling price of the pump is £1 078. Prepare a job cost to show the profit or loss on the job.
You are given the following information.

	A	B	C	D
Raw materials	£89	£134	£63	£206
Direct labour	£31	£28	£41	£74
Direct labour hours	10	8	12	33
Machine hours	—	4	—	12
Overhead recovery rates:				
Direct labour hour	£5	£6	£6	£5
Machine hour	—	£15	—	£13

5.2 You manufacture industrial fans, and a new accounting year has just commenced. A customer sends you an engineering drawing of a special fan to be used in a steel works. Delivery is required in six months' time, but the quotation must be submitted within three days. How will you prepare the quotation?

5.3 Quicksilver Products Ltd has incurred the following overhead charges in its various product and cost centres.

	£
Machine Shop	74 300
Electro-Plating Shop	67 200
Assembly Shop	84 700
Canteen	18 000
Maintenance Department	17 000
Stores	14 000
Depreciation	20 000
Rent and rates	24 000

You have been supplied with the following information:

	Number of employees	Maint. hours	Stores reqs.	Value of machinery	Floor Area (m^2)	Cubic capacity
Machine Shop	30	3 100	2 700	£94 000	1 000	15 000
Electro-Plating Shop	20	1 700	2 100	£39 000	800	4 000
Assembly Shop	60	3 950	5 200	£67 000	1 400	8 400
Canteen	10	—	—	—	—	—
Maintenance Department	6	—	—	—	—	—
Stores	4	200	—	—	—	—
Depreciation	—	—	—	—	—	—
Rent and Rates	—	—	—	—	—	—
	130	8 950	10 000	£200 000	3 200	27 400

	Direct labour hours	Machine hours
Machine Shop	39 035	10 811
Electro-Plating Shop	43 325	9 522
Assembly Shop	50 640	13 267
	133 000	33 600

Calculate overhead recovery rates for direct labour and machine hours, and express them to the nearest 1p.

6. Process Costing

Let us now consider the problems of process industries. All manufacturers do not produce single, one-off products, or small batches designed for a particular customer. Instead they have a continuous process of production, with raw materials passing through several processes before emerging finally as a finished product. One major difference between a job and process business is the variety of products that are produced. In a jobbing business many different variations of product are offered to customers. Often production cannot commence until an order has been received. Stocks of finished goods are low, as delivery is ensured on completion of production. A good example is a manufacturer of industrial fans, whose products will range from small ventilation fans to the huge giants that remove gases from, or provide the blast to, steelmaking furnaces. In a process business there will be fewer different products, but the quantities produced of each will be much greater. An oil refinery is a good example of a process business. The crude oil passes through several processes or distillations, with a different product resulting from each process.

(1) Overhead Allocation and Cost Build-up.

With job costing, costs are allocated to each individual job. With process costing allocation is only to a process. Direct materials when issued from the stores, or when purchased specially, will be allocated to a process. Direct labour will work for a specific process during the period for which that process is operating. There will be no need to keep time records, as there was with job costing. Changes will only take place when a new product passes through the process, and all employees will change at the same time. Overheads provide a bigger problem, but not as complex as in the case of job costing. The collection of overheads will take place through cost and product centres as before. The cost centres will represent the service side of the business. The product centres will correspond with the separate processes involved in production. After the initial allocation a re-allocation will be necessary, to transfer from the cost centres to the product or process centres. The principles of re-allocation will be similar to those used in job costing.

It is necessary to record accurately the numbers of items passing through each process. The numbers will vary from process to process due to:

(*a*) The numbers that are required from each process. Different numbers of sub-assemblies may be required to assemble into a finished product.

(*b*) The effect of scrap.

(*c*) The movement of unfinished stock units at each stage of production.

Each process will have allocated to it all relevant direct and indirect costs. Each item passing through the process will collect its share of these costs, which then accompany it to subsequent processes. Finally it emerges as a finished article at the end of the production cycle.

The unit cost of each process is calculated by dividing the costs of the process by the number of units produced. Assume that the production passing through a centre is 100 000 units during a period, and the costs are as follows:

	£
Direct materials	59 000
Direct labour	21 000
Variable overheads	16 000
Fixed overheads	49 000
	£145 000

The unit cost will be $\dfrac{£145\ 000}{100\ 000}$ = £1.45 per unit.

(2) Equivalent Production

There is a complicating factor in that all production at the accounting date is not completed, but remains as work in progress. To arrive at the unit cost, it would be wrong to divide the total cost only by the number of finished items passing to the next stage, as this would ignore the effect of uncompleted items. These unfinished items will rarely be the same in number at the beginning and end of a period. The opening work in progress stock will represent a number of units which are partly complete. At the end of a period, there will be a different number of units, again partly complete. The partial completion percentage will now probably be different from that at the beginning of the period. The partly completed items must be converted into an equivalent number of completed units. If, for example, 3 000 units of stock are 30% complete, the equivalent, in fully finished units will be 3 000 × 30% = 900 units. The effort required to complete that production will be the equivalent of 3 000 × 70% = 2 100 completed units. The number of units started and completed in a period must be adjusted by the opening and closing stocks of equivalent production.

Example

22 000 units of production were completed during a month. The work in progress stock at the beginning of the month was 4 000 units, 40% complete, and at the end of the month 3 000 units, 20% complete. What was the equivalent production for the month?

	Units
Units started and completed during the month	
22 000 — 4 000	18 000
Equivalent production to complete opening stock	
4 000 × 60%	2 400
Equivalent production in closing work in progress stock	
3 000 × 20%	600
	21 000

The percentages of the opening and closing stocks actually completed during the month are the ones used in the above calculation.

As production passes from one process to the next, it takes with it the accumulated cost to date. As it emerges from the final process it should represent the final cost of the completed product.

Example

Ashtrays Ltd manufacture a standard ashtray, which passes through three departments, namely stamping, electro-plating and polishing. For the month of December 19-0 production and sales were:

Department	Opening stock	% complete	Value £	Completed/ sold	Closing stock	% complete
A	3 000	20	620	24 000	2 000	40
B	4 000	40	1 550	23 000	5 000	50
C	2 000	70	2 688	22 000	3 000	80
Finished goods	6 000	100	12 000	25 400	2 600	100

The unit costs in each department were:

	A	B	C
Material	£0.50	£0.05	£0.12
Labour	£0.20	£0.10	£0.13
Variable overheads	£0.10	£0.08	£0.04
Fixed overheads (total)	£4 840	£4 633	£5 362

Stock records are maintained on the basis of FIFO, variable costs have been stable for several months, and the finished product sells for £2.50 per unit. All costs are stocked.

REQUIRED:
(a) Find the cost of one unit of finished production for the month.
(b) Calculate the profit on the sales for the month.

The first task is to calculate the equivalent production.

	A	B	C
Units completed and transferred	24 000	23 000	22 000
Less Opening stock W.I.P.	3 000	4 000	2 000
	21 000	19 000	20 000
Add Equivalent production to complete opening stock	2 400	2 400	600
Equivalent production of closing stock	800	2 500	2 400
	24 200	23 900	23 000

As FIFO is used for stock recording purposes, closing stock will be valued at the production cost of the month of December. The build up of cost throughout the departments will be:

			Closing stock	Value transferred
Department A:	£	£	£	£
Opening stock		620		
Material	12 100			
Labour	4 840			
Variable overheads	2 420			
Fixed overheads	4 840	24 200		
		£24 820	£800	£24 020

(Closing Stock = $\dfrac{800}{24\,200} \times £24\,200$)

Department B:				
Opening stock		1 550		
Transfer — Dept. A	24 020			
Material	1 195			
Labour	2 390			
Variable overheads	1 912			
Fixed overheads	4 633	34 150		
		£35 700	£3 572	£32 128

(Closing Stock = $\dfrac{2\,500}{23\,900} \times £34\,150$)

Department C:				
Opening stock		2 688		
Transfer — Dept. B	32 128			
Material	2 760			
Labour	2 990			
Variable overheads	920			
Fixed overheads	5 362	44 160		
		£46 848	£4 608	£42 240

(Closing Stock = $\dfrac{2\,400}{23\,000} \times £44\,160$)

The cost per unit of finished stock is calculated by dividing the cost of production for the month transferred to finished goods stock, by the number of units transferred, i.e.

$$\frac{£42\,240}{22\,000} = £1.92$$

	Closing Stock	Cost of Sales
Finished Goods:	£	£	£
Opening stock	12 000		
Add Production transferred	42 240		
	£54 240	£4 992	£49 248

(Closing Stock = $\frac{2\,600}{22\,000} \times £42\,240$)

The profit for the month can then be simply calculated:

	£
Sales (25 400 × £2.50)	63 500
Less Cost of sales	49 248
Profit	£14 252

It will be noted that the opening stock was valued at £2 per unit, and the production of the month at £1.92. With this information it is possible to prove the profit for the month. As FIFO is in operation, the whole of the opening stock is deemed to have been sold, and the profit will be:

	£
6 000 units @ £0.50 (£2.50 − £2.00)	3 000
19 400 units @ £0.58 (£2.50 − £1.92)	11 252
Total profit	£14 252

Assignments

6.1. In what ways does process costing differ from job costing?

6.2. Wirepens Ltd manufacture bird cages. During the month of January 19-0 the following production was recorded:

	Units
Opening stock of work in progress (45% complete)	5 000
Transferred to finished goods warehouse	24 000

Closing stock of work in progress (65% complete)   4 000
Calculate the equivalent production for the month.

6.3. Patream Ltd. commenced business on 1st. January 19-0 as manufacturers of a patented reamer. The accounting year ends on 31st December. During the three years to 31st December 19-2, its production was:

Year	Finished in year	Quarter-finished at year end	Sales during year
19-0	20 000	3 000	19 000
19-1	30 000	2 000	26 000
19-2	40 000	2 800	42 000

Throughout the three years, unit manufacturing costs were:

	£
Raw materials	4
Direct labour	3
Variable overheads	2

Fixed overheads were:

	£
19-0	103 750
19-1	119 000
19-2	120 600

It is the policy of the company to value finished and part-finished reamers on the basis of prime cost plus variable overheads, and a proportion of fixed overheads based on the number of units manufactured in each year. The FIFO system of stock valuation is used.

REQUIRED:
At the end of each of the three years, calculate the value of:
(a) The stock of finished reamers.
(b) The work in progress stock.

6.4. Eversharp Cutlery Ltd manufacture table knives. All production passes through the three departments, A, B and C. Stock records are kept on the FIFO basis.
Production records for June 19-1 were:

Department	Opening stock	% complete	Value £	Sold/ completed	Closing stock	% complete
A	1 000	20	220	12 000	2 000	40
B	1 500	50	1 200	13 000	500	30
C	2 000	60	2 200	14 000	1 000	70
Finished goods	7 000	100	12 600	18 000	3 000	100

The unit and other costs in each department were:

	A	B	C
Material (per unit)	£0.40	£0.10	£0.08
Labour (per unit)	£0.25	£0.20	£0.14
Variable overheads (per unit)	£0.20	£0.05	£0.03
Fixed overheads	£3 171	£1 628	£1 909

The knives are sold for £2.30 each.

REQUIRED:
(a) What was the cost of one unit of the finished product for the month?
(b) Calculate the profit on sales for the month.

7. Marginal Costing

Management accountants differ on the best method of preparing a cost statement. There are advocates of the absorption costing method. They believe that the best method of calculating the cost of a product is to allocate to it as many costs as can justifiably be supported. As has already been seen (Chapter 4), this requires a considerable amount of 'guesstimation' which cannot be altogether accurate.

There is a great difference between the various elements of cost, and the way in which they react to increases or falls in production. Direct, or prime, costs — materials, labour and some expenses — will vary completely with production. The unit cost will always remain the same regardless of the volume produced. The higher the production, the greater the overall total cost, and conversely with lower production.

Many of the overheads will be entirely different in character. They will remain fixed over a wide range of production. Take, for example, the rent of premises. This will be the same whether the business is operating at 1% or 100% of capacity. Similarly with heating and lighting. The bill will only be affected by the level of production if more shifts are engaged, requiring heating and lighting for longer periods. One works manager will be required for the whole factory. Together with his foremen, he will be able to control a wide range of production and labour.

Then there are semi-variable costs which have a fixed and variable element in them. Electricity charges, for example, will have a standing charge for KVA and a variable element for unit usage. Even then, units are not completely variable, as they only vary generally in line with production. A further example is a productivity bonus paid to supervisory and management staff. Basic salary will be a fixed overhead, while the bonus element will be variable. The variable costs will be separated from the fixed costs, and included under the appropriate category of overhead.

The fixed overheads will be roughly static in total cost. The unit costs, however, will vary considerably with production. The production of just one unit more or less, will vary the unit cost by some amount, no matter how small. Thus the behaviour of fixed and variable costs are completely contrary to each other. Absorption costing supporters claim that these entirely different elements of costs can be linked together in one product cost. Interpretation of the financial results of a period then becomes rather complex.

Take the example of a business that is making one product, with the following variable costs per unit:

Materials	£0.50
Labour	£0.30
Variable expenses	£0.20
Total variable cost	£1.00

The fixed overheads are £60 000. All costs remain static for a period of three years. In the first year production is 60 000 units; in the second year 90 000 units; in the third year 70 000 units. In each year sales of 60 000 units are made, at £2 per unit.
The costs will vary as follows.

	Year 1	Year 2	Year 3
Variable cost	£ 60 000	£ 90 000	£ 70 000
Fixed overhead	£ 60 000	£ 60 000	£ 60 000
	£120 000	£150 000	£130 000
Units produced	60 000	90 000	70 000
Unit cost	£ 2.00	£ 1.67	£ 1.86

Valuing the annual sales on the basis of the above costs, the trading results will vary as follows:

Sales	£120 000	£120 000	£120 000
Less Cost of sales	£120 000	100 200	111 600
Profit	—	£19 800	£ 8 400

With the same sales levels, three different results have been achieved. Imagine how to explain these differing results to a managing director not conversant with the niceties of accounting practice! If, however, marginal costing principles are applied, the results will be:

	Year 1	Year 2	Year 3
Sales	£120 000	£120 000	£120 000
Less Marginal cost	£ 60 000	£ 60 000	£ 60 000
Contribution	£ 60 000	£ 60 000	£ 60 000
Less Fixed overheads	£ 60 000	£ 60 000	£ 60 000
Profit	—	—	—

This is much easier to explain, as there is a constant relationship between sales and profit each year. The apparent profit under absorption costing is the result of stocking, and carrying forward, a varying element of fixed overheads.

Now examine the result of the application of absorption costing principles to sales policy decisions.

ABCo is a business making one product. During the year to 31st December 19-0 it manufactured 50 000 units which were all sold. Its overall costs were:

	£
Materials	30 000
Direct wages	28 000
Variable overheads	14 000
Fixed overheads	40 000

Its unit costs were:

	£
Materials	0.60
Direct wages	0.56
Variable overheads	0.28
Fixed overheads	0.80
	2.24

The unit selling price was £2.50, giving a profit of 26p per unit, or £13 000 for the total output of the year.

The sales manager then announced that a competitor had dropped the price for a similar product to £2.20, as a result of which sales were estimated to fall to 30 000 units per annum. The variable costs and fixed overheads were expected to remain static, and the unit cost would then increase.

		£
Variable cost (as before)		1.44
Fixed overheads	$\frac{£40\,000}{30\,000}$	1.33
		2.77

The absorption costing technique suggests that the price must be raised to at least £2.77, merely to break even. The sales manager could then justifiably claim that the result of such a move would be to lose most of the turnover, leaving the business no alternative but to close down.

If the price were dropped to £2.10 per unit, the sales manager explained, it would be possible to sell 70 000 units. Let us now examine the marginal costing concept, to see how it can help solve this apparent dilemma.

The many advocates of marginal costing claim that it is a much simpler concept than absorption costing. They claim that it is wrong to try to incorporate in one cost, both variable and fixed costs. The latter are very difficult to allocate to a product except by the application of arbitrary techniques. Why, therefore, try? Merely allocate variable costs to the product, and leave all fixed expenses as one unallocated lump. The difference between variable or marginal cost, and selling price, is called contribution. Management's objective will be to obtain sufficient contribution to exceed the fixed overheads, thus leaving a balance of profit. The contribution would be calculated:

		£
Direct materials	(70 000 × £0.60)	42 000
Direct wages	(70 000 × £0.56)	36 200
Variable overheads	(70 000 × £0.28)	16 600
Marginal cost		100 800
Contribution		46 200
Sales value	(70 000 × £2.10)	£147 000

52 Accounting for Management

With fixed overheads remaining at £40 000, an overall net profit of £7 000 would result.

If, by dropping the selling price to £2.00, 100 000 units could be sold, the result would be even more promising.

		£
Marginal cost (100 000 × £1.44)		144 000
Sales (100 000 × £2.00)		200 000
Contribution		56 000
Less Fixed overheads		40 000
Net profit		£16 000

The marginal costing approach is, therefore, much more flexible and useful than absorption costing. Its big disadvantage is that it gives no indication of what the selling price of a product should be. On the other hand, that is determined by market factors, and not the cost of the product.

The marginal technique is invaluable when deciding whether to accept work at less than normal selling price. Generally it is advisable to accept if the selling price is above marginal cost. This will give an added contribution which, unless fixed overheads increase, can only improve the overall profit, or decrease the overall loss.

Take the case of JCS which manufactures three products, A, B and C. The relevant information is:

	A	B	C
Variable cost	£1.40	£1.70	£2.10
Selling price	£2.10	£2.45	£3.00
Quantity sold	20 000	18 000	29 000
Fixed overheads		£45 000	

A customer has offered the following additional business, but at less than the normal selling prices. There is one proviso — the package must be accepted as a whole.

Product A	2 000 units @ £1.25
Product B	3 000 units @ £2.10
Product C	4 000 units @ £2.45

As a result of accepting the order, fixed overheads will increase by £2 000.

The profit on existing business is:

Marginal Costing

	A	B	C
Quantity	20 000	18 000	29 000
Variable cost	£28 000	£30 600	£60 900
Contribution	£14 000	£13 500	£26 100
Sales	£42 000	£44 100	£87 000

Total contribution
(£14 000 + £13 500 + £26 100)   £53 600
Less Fixed overheads   £45 000

Existing net profit   £ 8 600

The extra business, if accepted, will give the following additional contribution.

	A	B	C
Quantity	2 000	3 000	4 000
Variable cost	£2 800	£5 100	£8 400
Contribution	(£ 300)	£1 200	£1 400
Sales	£2 500	£6 300	£9 800

Total contribution
((£300) + £1 200 + £1 400)   £2 300
Less Increased fixed overheads   2 000

Extra profit   £ 300

It will, therefore, be advantageous to accept the extra order. Although product A will yield a negative contribution, it is swamped by the positive contributions arising on the other two products.

Fixed overheads rise in steps, and it would be pointless to take on extra work that would result in an increase in a large item of fixed overhead which would more than cancel out the extra contribution. If enlarged premises were required, their acquisition could only be justified if there were definite prospects of further substantial orders, making the project viable in the near future.

When a business is bursting at the seams and in urgent need of additional premises, a good, short-term measure to improve profitability is to try to replace poor-contribution work with that yielding a better contribution. The same applies when there is any other factor limiting the expansion of the business. It may, for example, be a lack of skilled labour; non-availability of suitable machinery; a shortage of raw materials. It will be necessary to concentrate on those jobs giving the greatest contribution in relation to expenditure on the resource that is in short supply.

Assignments

7.1 What are the advantages and disadvantages of absorption costing?

7.2 What are the advantages and disadvantages of marginal costing?

7.3 Explain, with examples, why the profit declared using an absorption costing system differs from that declared when using a marginal costing system.

7.4 Doom & Despair Ltd use an absorption costing system, in which selling price is calculated at total cost plus 10%. A single product is manufactured, and the unit cost, at a production level of 100 000 units is:

	£
Raw material	0.80
Direct labour	0.60
Variable overhead	0.40
Fixed overhead	0.50
Total cost	2.30
Add Profit @ 10%	0.23
Selling price	2.53

The sales director has requested an emergency board meeting to discuss the effect of foreign competition which has introduced a similar product selling for £2 per unit. Turnover for the coming year will drop by 50% if the present selling price is maintained. If the price were reduced to £2, the present sales level could be maintained. With a selling price of £1.90, sales would increase to 140 000 units a year. At all sales levels fixed overheads are expected to remain constant.

The purchasing director then announced that at levels of

sales above 130 000 a year, he could buy in bulk and make savings of 10p on the material cost of all units produced.

The managing director considers that the selling price should continue to be fixed as in the past, and seeks your advice.

What course of action do you recommend?

7.5 A business manufactures a single product which has a marginal cost of £1, sells for £2, and gives a contribution of £1 per unit. The fixed overheads of the organisation are £500 000 per annum. At present 480 000 units are being produced and sold. Maximum capacity is 550 000 units.

A salesman has prospects of an order, on a recurring basis, of 100 000 units per annum, at a price of £1.50 per unit. An adjacent factory is available for rental, with capacity to produce 200 000 extra units per annum. It will give rise to extra fixed overheads of £50 000 per annum.

As management accountant to the firm, you are required to prepare a report, advising on the best course of action, and taking into consideration all relevant factors.

8. Standard Costing

Standard costing is an aid to management. The various types of costing that have been illustrated to date have been based upon historical cost. Events that have already happened are incorporated into costs at the end of an accounting period. No attempt has been made to measure the efficiency — or lack of it — in the production process. If costs are too high, it will only be apparent when the overall cost is compared with the selling price, and a poor profit, or even a loss, is shown. Even then, the information gained is not very informative. No indication is given about which element of cost, or which part of the production process, is too high.

This is where a system of standard costing can be of use. A standard cost is an estimate of the cost of doing a job in advance of actual production. It is a measuring rod used to assess the efficiency of production. The standard is set in the following manner.

(*a*) The usage of raw material is estimated from engineering drawings. The price expected to be paid for those materials is estimated from a knowledge of future market trends.

(*b*) The method of manufacture of the job will be determined, and the time to be taken estimated. The expected labour rates, taking into consideration future government wages policy, and impending wage negotiations, will be applied to the estimated time. This will give the standard labour cost. When estimating the time content of a job, it is important to ensure that a time is set that can be achieved by a reasonably competent employee, working in a conscientious manner. If the standard is not attainable, no effort will be made to try to achieve it. Similarly if it is too easily achieved, lethargy will set in on the shop floor, and no attempt will be made to improve productivity.

(c) The standard overhead content of a job is arrived at from a budget. A budget is an estimate, made in advance, of what expenditure, under the various accounting headings, there will be in a future period, usually twelve months. Budgeting will be dealt with in greater detail in Chapters 10 and 11. Briefly, in preparing the budget, attention must be paid to the following points:

(i) Expenditure that has been incurred in the past year.
(ii) Any changes due to take place, such as increasing the number of shifts to be worked, or moving into new premises.
(iii) The effect of any anticipated price adjustments.
(iv) The level of future production.
(v) The numbers and grades of employees during the coming year.

From this information it will be possible to produce an overheads budget for the period. The sales budget will indicate the various products that will be produced during the year. The sales budget, adjusted by stock movements, will give the production budget. From this a labour hours budget can be constructed. If required a machine hours budget can also be prepared. These will then provide a vehicle for loading the overheads onto the cost of jobs being manufactured. They form a basis for calculating the overhead recovery rate, either based upon direct labour hours, or machine hours.

From the above information it should be possible to prepare a standard cost for any product. Actual costs can be compared with it. If there are any differences between the two — and there usually are — the reasons can be analysed. The usual bases of analysis are price and volume. Variances will arise because prices actually paid have differed from those used in the standard cost; and the volume of production will vary from the levels incorporated in the standard.

Budgets are important for standard costing, and it would be impossible to prepare standard costs if no budgets were produced. On the other hand, as we shall see in later chapters, it would still be possible to have a budget without preparing standard costs.

Standard costs have several advantages.

(a) Although they take much time to prepare, they can remain unchanged for periods up to a year. Thereafter they can be adjusted in the light of price and other changes.

(b) The task of budgeting, and the preparation of standard costs, can bring to light many points of inefficiency in an organisation.

(c) They provide a useful tool for measuring the efficiency of an organisation.

(d) After the preparation of the standard costs, the costing system is more easily run. Production is evaluated at the standard material, labour and overhead content, and compared with actual charges in total. There is no need to analyse all costs to each individual job or process, as in the case of an historical costing system.

(e) Faster reporting usually results from the adoption of standard costing. The analysis element in book-keeping can be reduced.

(f) Standard costing is a versatile system. Although standard costs get out of date with price increases, it is possible to apply simple percentage adjustments to bring them into line with actual costs. Estimating the cost of future jobs, for sales estimate purposes, then becomes easy.

In the present cold economic climate management must have as much information as possible about its financial results. A standard cost is a well thought out idea of the cost of a job, and any variation from that in actual performance should be investigated immediately. Rectifying action can then be taken as soon as possible.

Variance Analysis

Once standard costs have been calculated, they are of immense benefit to management in its task of monitoring efficiency. As soon as the production of a period is known, the standard cost of that production can be calculated. Before actual costs are available, management will already know what to expect, and if the actual results differ too much from standard, investigations can be commenced into the reasons.

Variance analysis aims to analyse the differences between standard and actual results, in order that the areas of difference can be more easily spotlighted. Let us confine our attention to the prime costs of production — direct materials and direct labour. Variances are always based upon the total actual production of the period. How much should it have cost to produce the production of the period, if all costs had been at standard levels? How much has it actually cost to produce? The variances that result may be either favourable or adverse. Start always with the standard cost of production — the cost that was expected to be incurred. If actual cost is higher than standard, the variance will be adverse. If it is less than standard, the variance will be favourable.

The principles can be illustrated from the following example. Stanco Ltd manufactures a single product, and operates a system of standard costing. The standard unit cost is:

  Materials 3 kilogrammes @ £1 per kilogramme
  Labour   2 hours @ £2.50 per hour

During January 19-7, 5 000 units were produced. The overall costs were:

  Materials 18 000 kilogrammes @ £0.90 per kilogramme
  Labour   9·000 hours @ £2.80 per hour

Calculate separately the material and labour variances.

Material Variances

Differences between standard and actual cost can arise for two reasons.

(a) The price of materials has differed.
(b) The usage of those materials has varied.

(i) *Material Price Variance* This is calculated by evaluating actual production at standard material price and comparing it with the actual material price. The variance is the difference between standard and actual price on all the material used. In the case of Stanco:

		£
Standard	18 000 kg @ £1.00	18 000
Actual	18 000 kg @ £0.90	16 200
Favourable variance		£1 800

(ii) *Material Usage Variance* This compares the standard usage of material and the actual usage, both at standard price. The variance is the difference in usage valued at standard material cost.

		£
Standard	5 000 × 3 × £1	15 000
Actual	18 000 @ £	18 000
Adverse variance		£3 000

Accounting for Management

Labour Variances

As with material variances, there are two principal reasons for differences between standard and actual labour costs.

(*a*) The hourly wage rate has varied from standard.
(*b*) The rate of production has differed from that expected when the standards were compiled.

(i) *Labour Rate Variances* This shows the difference in cost that has arisen because the wage rate paid for actual production has not been at the standard level expected. The variance is the difference in wage rate applied to all the hours worked to achieve the production. In the Stanco example:

		£
Standard	9 000 @ £2.50	22 500
Actual	9 000 @ £2.80	25 200
Adverse variance		£2 700

(ii) *Labour Efficiency Variance* This compares the standard hours required for the production of the period with the hours actually needed. Both are evaluated at standard wage rate. The variance represents the difference between the hours that should have been worked to obtain the production and those actually worked, evaluated at the standard wage rate.

		£
Standard	5 000 × 2 h × £2.50	25 000
Actual	9 000 @ £2.50	22 500
Favourable variance		£2 500

Presenting the Information

The variances have now been calculated, but they must be organised in a logical manner that will help management in its task of running the business. It was expected that production would have been at standard. In fact it has varied from this. The two sets of figures must be reconciled to show the reasons for the discrepancy.

	Material	Labour	Total
	£	£	£
Standard cost of production	15 000	25 000	40 000
Material variances — Price	(1 800)	—	(1 800)
— Usage	3 000	—	3 000
Labour variances — Rate	—	2 700	2 700
Efficiency	—	(2 500)	(2 500)
Actual cost of production	£16 200	£25 200	£41 400

Note that adverse variances increase standard cost, while favourable ones reduce it.

This statement will now be pointing towards avenues of investigation to discover the reasons for the excessive costs. Material price variance is favourable, but usage is adverse. This could be the result of buying cheap but inferior materials which have caused wastage. Labour variances also suggest this. Wage rate variance is adverse, suggesting that a higher grade of labour was used on the job. Efficiency, although better than standard, was not sufficiently high to cover the adverse rate variance. This could have been due to material quality problems. This is one avenue of investigation to pursue. On the other hand, the adverse wage rate variance may be due simply to a higher than expected wage settlement. Adverse efficiency could have resulted from industrial action before negotiations were concluded.

Already several areas of exploration are opening up. Each will be explored until the right answer is known. The organisation will become gradually more efficient. Yet, without standard costing, it is doubtful if management would even have suspected the existence of a problem.

Assignments

8.1. How far can a system of standard costing be prepared without first budgeting?

8.2. At a board meeting the sales director is pressing for the adoption of strict standards in order to lower selling prices. The works director wants loose standards to keep his labour force happy. The managing director asks for your opinion. Advise him.

62 Accounting for Management

8.3. What are the advantages of a standard costing system?

8.4. In what ways is variance analysis a useful management technique?

8.5. Arrantex Ltd, manufacturers of knitted sweaters, have decided to instal a system of standard costing. The following standard unit costs have been agreed:
    Materials   1½ kg wool @ £2 per kg
    Labour   3 hours @ £1.80 per hour
During the month of June 19-3, 3 000 sweaters were produced at the following actual costs:
    Materials   4 800 kg wool @ £1.95 per kg
    Labour   9 400 hours @ £1.50 per hour
Prepare a report showing the efficiency of production during the month.

Part II
Forecasts and Budgets

9. Sampling and Forecasting Techniques

It is now necessary to look at some of the statistical techniques that can be used in the preparation of budgets. A budget is an estimate of what future results are likely to be, and full use must be made of all techniques that can help to make that forecast accurate.

Survey and Census Techniques

The dominant factor in any budget is the size of the demand for the product. Survey and census techniques can help greatly in deciding what the demand will be. If the business is producing a consumer product, information will be required from the general public. If a product is produced that is sold to other manufacturers, the survey will be confined to actual or potential industrial customers. In the second case a full census could be taken, especially if the extent of the market is not great. Information required from the general public can best be obtained by means of sampling. This is a technique based on the law of statistical regularity, which states that a set taken from a larger group will reproduce the characteristics of that larger group. There are some exceptions, especially where some items in the larger group are much larger than the rest. It is then best to compare several samples. Generally speaking, the larger the sample, the greater will be its resemblance to the population from which it is taken.

Whichever method is chosen will depend on:
(a) The cost in time and money.
(b) The speed with which the results are required.
(c) The degree of accuracy required.

The cost of a sample will be much less than a full-scale census, the results will be available more quickly, and it is possible to obtain a wider spread of information. A decision must be taken on the best method of carrying out the survey. Two methods are usually employed — the postal survey and the interview. The former is most frequently used, but it suffers from a high non-response rate. On the other hand it allows plenty of time to consider the answer. With trained interviewers a high response rate is assured, yet interviewer bias can emerge where a reply is misunderstood, or a wrong code number is used by the interviewer on his schedule. Response errors may result from faulty memory, or a desire to impress the interviewer.

Questionnaires

A good questionnaire is vital to a sound and successful survey. It must:

(a) be clear, and expressed in clear language.
(b) be free from ambiguity.
(c) be set out in a logical order.
(c) lead the respondent to answer truthfully and intelligently.

Leading questions and emotive words must always be excluded.

The following is a sample questionnaire for an electric razor survey, designed for the male element in the community.

ELECTRIC RAZOR SURVEY	
(1) Do you own an electric razor?	Yes/No
(2) If so, what make is it?	....
If not, proceed to question 9.	
(3) How long have you had it?	Under 6 months
(Please tick)	6 – 12 months
	1 year
	2 years
	3 years
	4 years
	5 years
	Over 5 years
(4) Did you buy it yourself?	Yes/No
If no, was it a present?	Yes/No

(5) At what sort of shop did you buy it?   Department store
    (Please tick)   Electrical shop
                                           Barber's shop
                                           Chemist shop
                                           Wholesaler
                                           Other
(6) Have you had it repaired in the last 6
    months?   Yes/No
(7) Do you have a moustache, or other
    facial hair, that requires trimming?   Yes/No
(8) Do you use pre-electric shaving lotion? Yes/No
(9) What do you consider is a fair price for
    an electric razor?   ....
(10) Is there anything you particularly
     dislike about electric shavers?   ....
(11) What is your age group?   16 – 24
     (Please tick)   25 – 34
                                           35 – 44
                                           45 – 59
                                           60 +
(12) Name ....
     Address ....
                                           Post code ....
(13) Region ....
(14) Investigation Number ....

Before carrying out the main survey a pilot survey is often undertaken, with the objective of testing that the questionnaire is well designed and as near fool-proof as possible. Some useful information may also emerge, such as the scale of the non-response, but that will not be the main objective of the survey.

Types of Sample

The sample is then selected from the sampling frame. This is a listing of the whole population about which it is desired to obtain information. In the case of a business, selling to other businesses, it will be a complete, up-to-date list of actual and potential customers. A business that is selling to the public could use the Electoral Register as its sampling frame.

There are several methods of selecting the sample, but the five most common are:

(a) *Random Sampling* With this method the sample is chosen in a manner whereby each member of the population not yet chosen has an equal chance of being selected. All items in the population will be numbered, and the sample chosen by using a table of random numbers. This table will be compiled by means of a random process. This is not the same as a haphazard selection, and if the sampling frame is sound the sample will be completely unbiased.

(b) *Stratified Sampling* This requires a prior knowledge of the population. The sampling frame is divided into sections or strata, which may be regions, towns, suburbs, streets, age groups, sexes etc. depending on the nature of the investigation. Within each region, such as the Midlands, North of England or Wales, a random sample of towns is taken, and then within each town a random sample of customers, of the required size, is taken. The method ensures that each section of the overall population is represented, and it is much more economical than random sampling. Field staff can concentrate on a limited number of areas, thus cutting down on the amount of travelling involved.

(c) *Cluster Sampling* This is similar to stratified sampling, but instead of taking a sample within a sub-stratum, the whole of the sub-stratum is taken. It is really a full sample at the final stage of a multi-stage sample. This type of sampling is useful where the variation within clusters is larger than that among clusters, and also where no comprehensive sampling frame for the whole population exists.

(d) *Quota Sampling* This is like non-random stratified sampling. The total sample within each selected area is completely broken down, but the interviewer is allowed complete discretion of choice of the people interviewed. There is a danger of bias creeping in, but it is a cheap and easy method, requiring no sampling frame and no calls back. It is, however, impossible to place estimates of reliability on this sampling method.

(e) *Systematic Sampling* The sample is taken in a systematic manner, usually by taking items at regular intervals. A random list of actual and potential customers can be numbered, and a sample taken by choosing say, every tenth number. The method is virtually as good as the random method.

Sample Mean and Standard Deviation

When the sampling method has been chosen, and the sample taken, it will be necessary to decide on the accuracy of the results. How near to the results of the sample can the overall results be expected to be? The first stage in calculating this is to arrive at the mean of the sample. The mean (symbol $\bar{x}$) is the arithmetic average of all items in the sample. It is calculated by dividing the total (symbol Σx) by the number of items (symbol n). The formula is:

$$\bar{x} = \frac{\Sigma x}{n}$$

Example

A sample of ten customers gives the following estimated sales requirement for the coming year.

	£'000
A	8
B	7
C	6
D	9
E	7
F	10
G	11
H	7
J	8
K	7

Calculate the mean.

Total sales will be £80 000, and the number of customers 10.

The mean will be $\dfrac{£80\ 000}{10}$ = £8 000 per customer.

With the mean it is possible to calculate the standard deviation. We know the average figure of expected sales per customer, but this does not tell us whether the individual figures are close together or

spread out. The standard deviation (symbol σ or sigma) is calculated by:
(i) Squaring the difference between the mean of the sample and the individual values.
(ii) Dividing this by the number of items in the sample.
(iii) Calculating the square root of the answer.
The formula is:

$$\sigma = \sqrt{\frac{\Sigma(x - \bar{x})^2}{n}}$$

Example

Calculate the standard deviation of the sample used above.

x (£'000)	$(x - \bar{x})$	$(x - \bar{x})^2$	$\bar{x}$
8	8 - 8 = 0	0	
7	7 - 8 = -1	1	
6	6 - 8 = -2	4	$\frac{80}{10} = 8$
9	9 - 8 = +1	1	
7	7 - 8 = -1	1	
10	10 - 8 = +2	4	
11	11 - 8 = +3	9	
7	7 - 8 = -1	1	
8	8 - 8 = 0	0	
7	7 - 8 = -1	1	
$x = 80$		$\Sigma(x - x)^2 = 22$	

$$\sigma = \sqrt{\frac{22}{10}} = \sqrt{2.2} = 1.484$$

Standard deviation = £1 484

The standard deviation indicates the spread of the distribution. As it is based upon correct mathematical processes, further calculations can be based upon it. In the above example one standard deviation from the mean will include values from £9 484 to £6 516 (£8 000 ± £1 484, the standard deviation).

Significance of the Sample Results

The information that has been calculated to date concerns the sample. It must now be decided how relevant this is to the population as a whole, and with what degree of accuracy the sample result can be used to forecast the result of the entire population. Statistical experience indicates that there is a normal curve of distribution in a set of figures. If it were plotted as a graph, there would be a higher incidence around the mean, rapidly falling away to both sides as one moves away from the mean. It is bell-shaped, symmetrical, the mean lies at the peak of the curve, and the two tails approach the horizontal axis without actually touching it. (See Fig. 9.1.)

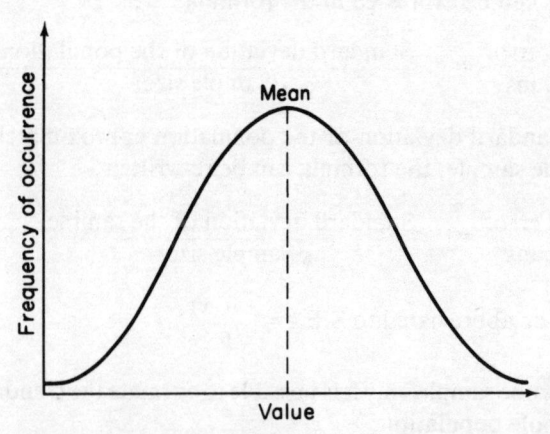

Fig. 9.1. *Curve of normal distribution*

Confidence Limits

Almost the entire area of a normal distribution curve lies within three standard deviations of the mean. The exact percentage is 99.74. Points plotted at two standard deviations either side of the mean will cover 95.44% of the area. Similar points plotted at one standard deviation either side of the mean will enclose 68.26% of the area. Reverting to the example above, we can state with confidence that 68.26% of the sales will fall between £9 484 and £6 516; 95.44% will fall between £10 968 and £5 032; and 99.74% will fall between £12 452 and £3 548.

Population Mean

An estimate of the population mean can be gained from the sample mean, which is known to be approximately that of the whole population, but it is not *exactly* so. Yet if the mean of all samples is plotted on a histogram, the curve will probably look very much like a rather slim version of a normal distribution curve. The number of items in a sample must be over forty if this is always to hold good. The standard deviation of these sample distributions can be found by calculating the standard deviation of each sample. This is a major task, and hardly worth the effort involved. There is, however, a connection between the standard deviation — or standard error — of the means, the standard deviation of the population, and the sample size. This can be expressed in the formula:

$$\text{Standard error of the means} = \frac{\text{Standard deviation of the population}}{\sqrt{\text{Sample size}}}$$

As the standard deviation of the population approximately equals that of the sample, the formula can be re-written

$$\text{Standard error of the means} = \frac{\text{Standard deviation of the sample}}{\sqrt{\text{Sample size}}}$$

This can be abbreviated to $\text{S.E.} = \frac{\sigma(x)}{\sqrt{n}}$

By taking one sample only it is possible to estimate the standard error of the whole population.

The standard error is a significant figure. It is known that in a normal distribution 95% of the items lie within two standard deviations of the mean of that distribution. Similarly in 19 out of 20 cases, the mean of a sample will lie within two standard errors of the population mean. In order to estimate the true mean of a population, take the mean of a sample, calculate the standard error, and then it can be stated with 95% accuracy that the true mean will be within two standard errors of the sample mean.

Example

Assume that the sample taken before had consisted of 40 items, and had given a mean of £8 000 and a standard deviation of £1 484. The standard error will be:

$$\frac{1\ 484}{\sqrt{40}} = \frac{1\ 484}{6.325} = £235$$

The true mean of the population, with 95% confidence, can be said to lie between £7 530 and £8 470. If a greater degree of confidence is required, say a certainty of 1 in 400, it will be necessary to extend to three standard errors, and state that the population mean will lie between £7 295 and £8 705. The confidence interval will be the distance between the confidence limits. In the above example, at 95% confidence level, the interval will be £940, but at the 99.74% level it will be £1 410. Thus, the higher the confidence level, the higher the confidence interval, and vice versa.

The sampling techniques used to date are not confined simply to the calculation of a sales budget. There are many other applications in industry. They can be used to calculate the mean weight of products from samples. This can be useful for budgeting purposes where the weight of material used is not accurately known. Its greatest use is for quality control, where the weight of a product must be held within defined tolerances. The methods can also be used when setting labour standards — the time taken to perform operations on the shop floor. Whatever the application, the methods are the same as those illustrated above.

Correlation

This is another useful statistical technique that can be used by the accountant for forecasting purposes. Its main use is in forecasting two variables between which there may, or may not, be a connection. The technique will show how close the connection is, and this information can then be used to predict and also control events. Of the two variables, one will be an independent variable, not affected by changes in the other; the other one will be the dependent variable, which is affected by changes in the other. Each set of variables must be considered on its merits. Take the case of sales and transport costs. It is usual for the vendor to be responsible for the transport of products to the customer. An increase in sales will result in an increase in transport costs. Conversely, an increase in transport costs does not necessarily indicate an increase in sales, as the increased costs may be due to a different distribution pattern, or an increase in operating costs.

Scatter Graphs

The correlation between two variables can be disclosed by the construction of a scatter graph in the following manner.

74 Accounting for Management

(a) Decide on the independent and dependent variables.

(b) Construct a graph in which the independent variable is plotted along the horizontal axis, and the dependent variable along the vertical axis.

(c) Plot each pair of variables as a single point on the graph.

(d) Enter the line of best fit. This is a straight line which represents the average line of the points plotted. The extension of this line will then enable a reading to be made of the transport costs for any forecast level of sales.

Example

The sales and transport costs of a business, for a five year period, are as follows:

	Sales £'000	Transport £'000
19-4	1 174	22
19-5	1 398	23
19-6	1 681	29
19-7	1 947	37
19-8	2 164	44

Construct a scatter graph, enter the line of best fit, and estimate the transport costs for 19-9, assuming sales will be £2 500 000.

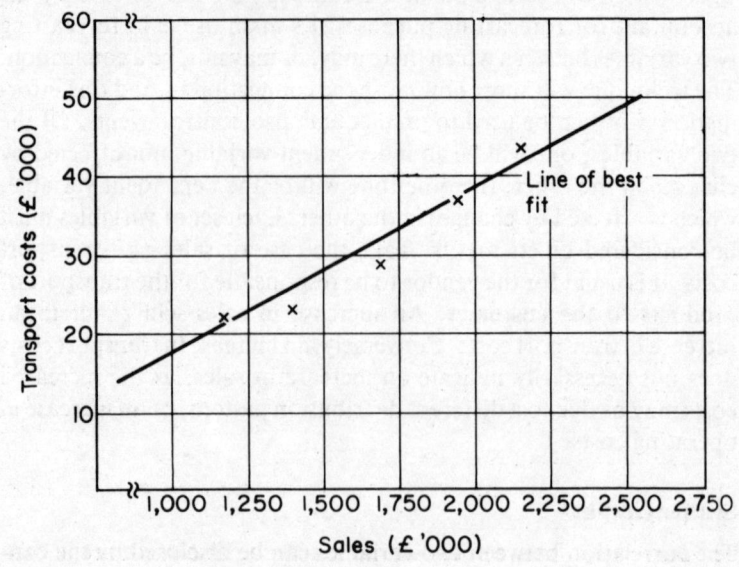

Fig. 9.2. *Scatter graph of sales/transport costs*

From the graph it can be seen that the expected transport costs for a turnover of £2 500 000 will be approximately £49 000.

The technique can be applied to several other aspects of forecasting, such as the relationship between sales and advertising expenditure; sales and travelling and entertaining expenditure; wages and salaries and employment expenses; production and consumable expenses, to name only a few.

Great care must be exercised in interpreting the results of a scatter graph. There will be a degree of uncertainty about the correct position of the line of best fit, and also about the degree of closeness of the relationship of the two variables. It is possible to obtain an idea of the correlation of the two variables from the closeness of the points plotted to the line of best fit.

(*a*) If the line rises from left to right, and all points are on the line of best fit, it is known as a perfect positive correlation.

(*b*) If the line falls from left to right, but all points plotted are on the line of best fit, it is known as a perfect negative correlation.

(*c*) If the pattern is the same as in (*a*) but the points are slightly offset from the line of best fit, it is known as a high positive correlation.

(*d*) If the pattern is the same as in (*b*) but the points are again slightly offset, it is known as a high negative correlation.

(*e*) If the pattern is as in (*c*) or (*d*), but the points are more offset from the line of best fit, it will represent a low positive or negative correlation.

(*f*) If the points are scattered everywhere, with no possibility of plotting a line of best fit, the variables are deemed to be uncorrelated.

The accuracy of the forecast derived from a scatter graph will depend upon the closeness of the points plotted to the line of best fit.

Time Series and Trends

The time series is another statistical method that can be used as an aid to forecasting. The values of many variables will change with the passage of time. In the business world there are sales, profits, production, usage of raw materials and numbers employed, to name only a few. The most important aspect of a time series that aids forecasting is the determination of a trend, or the general course that will be taken over a long period of time, assuming that there are no disturbing factors present. If a trend can be established from the past up to the present time, it is logical to assume that it will be continued into the future, in the absence of any outside disturbing factors. All businesses will have records of past performance, and from these a projection can be made into the future.

Example

Let us take the quarterly sales of Greetings Cards Ltd for the last four years, with the intention of forecasting turnover for the coming year.

Greetings Cards Ltd
Quarterly Sales in £'000

Year	Quarter 1	Quarter 2	Quarter 3	Quarter 4
19-8	120	160	180	210
19-9	130	180	200	240
19-0	140	200	230	270
19-1	160	230	260	300

The first thing that one notes is the seasonal variation in the figures. The first quarter of the year is always the lowest period for turnover. When the figures are plotted on a graph, a saw-toothed curve results.

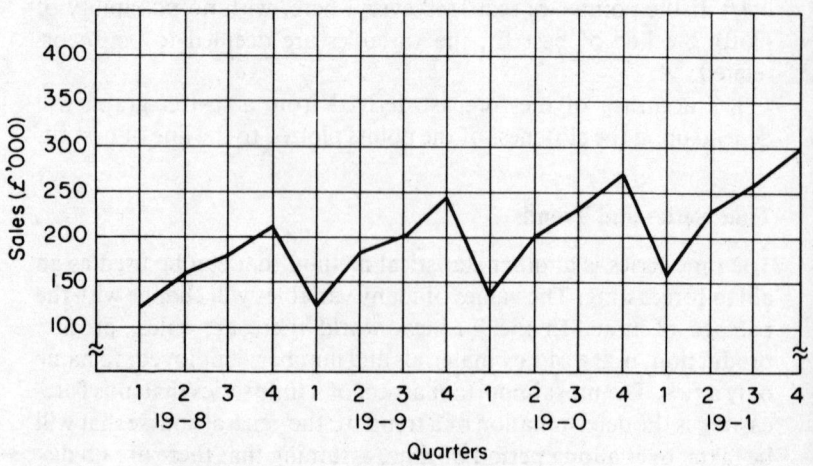

Fig. 9.3. *Greetings Cards Ltd — quarterly sales*

From this it is very difficult to plot a trend. In order to even out the irregularities, moving quarterly averages can be calculated.

(a) Add up the total sales of the first year, and divide by four.

(b) The sales of the first quarter of 19-8 are dropped and replaced by the corresponding figure for the first quarter of 19-9. This new total is again divided by four to give the second moving quarterly average.

(c) Continue each quarter up to the present time.

As the figures resulting from these calculations represent the average quarterly sales for a yearly period, they will be plotted on the graph at the mid-point of the period. The first moving average will lie at the end of June 19-8. Subsequent averages will be plotted at quarterly intervals

Table of quarterly moving averages

	Quarter	Actual sales	Moving annual total	Quarterly moving average
		£'000	£'000	£'000
19-8	1	120		
	2	160		
			670	167.5
	3	180		
			680	170.0
	4	210		
			700	175.0
19-9	1	130		
			720	180.0
	2	180		
			750	187.5
	3	200		
			760	190.0
	4	240		
			780	195.0
19-0	1	140		
			810	202.5
	2	200		
			840	210.0
	3	230		
			860	215.0
	4	270		
			890	222.5
19-1	1	160		
			920	230.0
	2	230		
			950	237.5
	3	260		
	4	300		

78 *Accounting for Management*

These quarterly moving averages are then plotted on a graph, with time recorded on the horizontal axis, and sales on the vertical one.

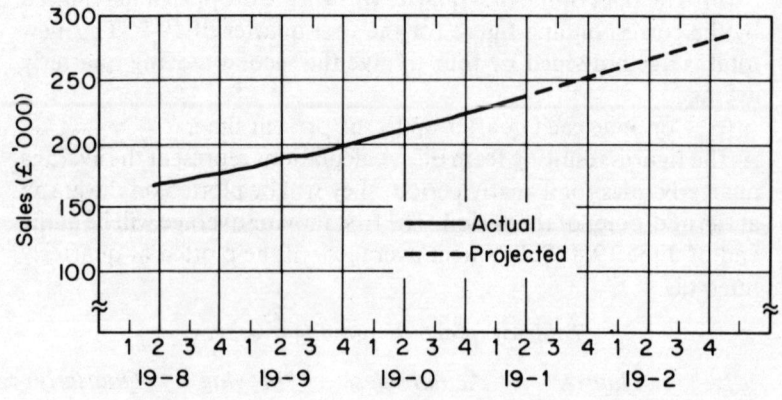

Fig 9.4. *Greetings Cards Ltd — quarterly sales moving average*

It will be noted that the seasonal fluctuations have now disappeared, and a much straighter line has been plotted. Estimates of future turnover can now be made by extending the line of the graph over the last two or three years, to show the estimated quarterly moving average sales of the coming year (broken line in the illustration). From a reading these will be:

	£
Quarter 1	245 000
Quarter 2	251 000
Quarter 3	257 000
Quarter 4	265 000
	£1 018 000

In the example there is a seasonal pattern to turnover. The first quarter of the year is always the poorest. This can make it difficult to compare one quarter with another, without causing confusion. The next task is to remove the seasonal variations.

Firstly each quarter's sales must be expressed as a percentage of the moving average. Thus in the third quarter of 19-8 it will be calculated as follows:

$$\frac{180.0}{167.5} \times 100 = 107\%$$

A similar calculation will follow for each subsequent quarter.

Table of sales as a percentage of moving average

Quarter		Sales £'000	Moving average £'000	Sales as a Percentage of Moving Average
19-8	1	120		
	2	160		
			167.5	107
	3	180		
			170.0	123
	4	210		
			175.0	74
19-9	1	130		
			180.0	100
	2	180		
			187.5	106
	3	200		
			190.0	126
	4	240		
			195.0	71
19-0	1	140		
			202.5	98
	2	200		
			210.0	109
	3	230		
			215.0	125
	4	270		
			222.5	71
19-1	1	160		
			230.0	100
	2	230		
			237.5	109
	3	260		
	4	300		

The seasonal factor can now be averaged for the period. The percentages for each quarter are totalled and divided by the number of items to give the averages. It is then necessary to adjust these averages so that the total adds up to 400, or 100 per quarter on the average.

Seasonal Factors

Year	Quarter 1	2	3	4	Total
19-8	—	—	107	123	
19-9	74	100	106	126	
19-0	71	98	109	125	
19-1	71	100	—	—	
Total	216	298	322	374	1 210
Average	71	99	107	123	400

These quarterly factors can now be applied to the quarterly sales for the period, to give seasonally adjusted sales. Taking the sales of the third quarter of 19-8, the adjusted figure will be:

$$\frac{180}{107} \times 100 = 168$$

The seasonally adjusted sales for this quarter will then be £168 000 instead of the actual figure of £180 000. Where sales are low, the seasonal factor will be a small percentage, and the seasonally adjusted figure will be higher. The reverse applies where seasonal sales are high.

Table of Quarterly Sales, Seasonally Adjusted

Quarter		Actual Sales £'000	Seasonal Factor %	Adjusted Sales £'000
19-8	1	120	71	169
	2	160	99	161
	3	180	107	168
	4	210	123	170
19-9	1	130	71	183
	2	180	99	182
	3	200	107	187
	4	240	123	195
19-0	1	140	71	197
	2	200	99	202
	3	230	107	215
	4	270	123	219
19-1	1	160	71	225
	2	230	99	232
	3	260	107	243
	4	300	123	244

Having removed the seasonal variation from the figures, they may be plotted on a graph (Fig. 9.5).

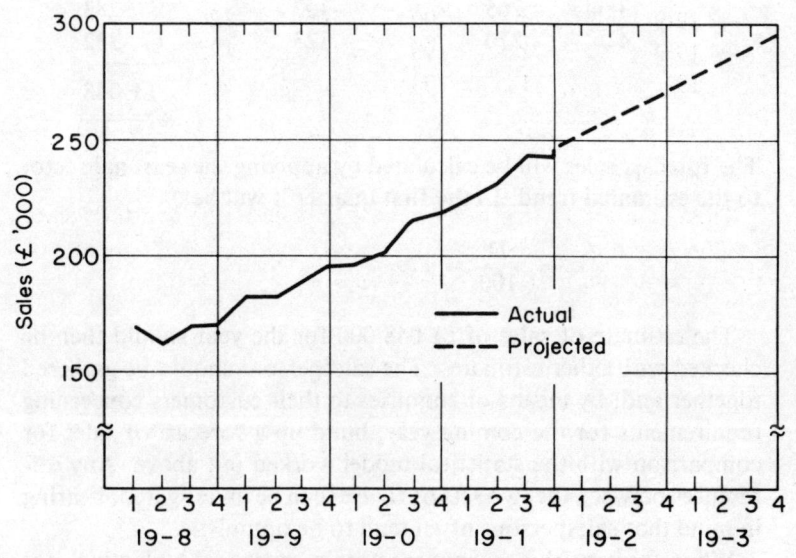

Fig. 9.5. *Sales adjusted for seasonal movements*

With the seasonal variations eliminated, the line is now much smoother, but not as smooth as the trend line. This indicates that there is still some random fluctuation left in the figures.

Forecasting the Future

All effort so far has been on preparing historical figures. The next stage is to look to the future, and try to gauge what future results will be. Whatever figures result will only be approximately accurate and only then if underlying conditions remain the same as in the past. Obviously, in the case of sales, if a major customer is lost during the coming year, it will adversely affect the sales performance.

With this proviso in mind, it will now be necessary to extend or extrapolate the trend from the last two or three years, by means of a straight line. To this must be applied the appropriate seasonal factor to give the quarterly forecast sales. In the example this could give rise to the following position.

Quarter		Estimated trend £'000	Seasonal factor %	Forecast sales £'000
19-2	1	252	71	179
	2	257	99	254
	3	265	107	283
	4	270	123	332
				£1 048

The forecast sales will be calculated by applying the seasonal factor to the estimated trend. In the first quarter it will be

$$252 \times \frac{71}{100} = 179.$$

The estimate of sales of £1 048 000 for the year should then be checked with other estimates. The salespersons should be gathered together and, by means of enquiries to their customers concerning requirements for the coming year, build up a forecast of sales for comparison with the statistical model worked out above. Any differences between the two sets of figures can be investigated, bearing in mind that salespersons often tend to be optimistic.

When applying this technique to other aspects of budgeting, it is imperative to adjust for exceptional happenings that may be entering or dropping out of the figures. In the case of production, if new equipment is being installed which has a much quicker production time, productivity will be much higher than in the past. Again, if gross profit is being estimated, but a new product is being introduced which has an especially low profit margin, the estimated results must be adjusted to take this factor into consideration.

Assignments

9.1. Prepare a sample questionnaire for a survey of the market for double glazing.

9.2. (i) What is a sample?
(ii) What are the main methods of selecting a sample?
(iii) Which method would you use to survey a nationwide, specialist market, when you are working within a very tight budget? Give your reasons.

Sampling and Forecasting Techniques 83

9.3. A machined part should weigh 81 grammes ± 6%. From the production of a shift thirty samples were selected at random, and weighed. The weights were:

81	82	83	80	78	80	81	79	82	80
81	81	83	81	83	82	79	78	80	81
82	78	79	81	83	78	79	81	82	80

Can you be virtually 100% certain that the production of the day is satisfactory? Show your workings.

9.4. A machine produces bars of chocolate which should weigh 55 grammes each. The mean weight of the bars may not vary by more than 1%. The quality controller is prepared to accept a 99% certainty that the machine is performing properly.

A sample of 50 bars has been weighed, and the standard deviation of the sample is 1.2 grammes.

(i) Is the production for the day acceptable?
(ii) Would there be any difference if the sample size had been 40 items only?

9.5. You are preparing an overheads budget for salespersons' travelling and entertainment expenses. The figures for the last four years, together with the relevant sales are:

	Sales	Travelling and entertainment
	£	£
19-1	2 800 000	7 000
19-2	3 200 000	8 000
19-3	3 800 000	9 600
19-4	4 300 000	11 200

The budgeted sales for 19-5 are £5 100 000.
By means of a scatter graph estimate the travelling and entertainment expenses for 19-5.

9.6. Tiger Ice Cream Ltd has maintained quarterly sales records for the past four years. They are:

84 Accounting for Management

Years	Quarters			
	(1) £	(2) £	(3) £	(4) £
19-0	200 000	260 000	500 000	180 000
19-1	220 000	300 000	600 000	210 000
19-2	250 000	360 000	690 000	230 000
19-3	260 000	390 000	740 000	270 000

(a) Calculate the quarterly moving average sales.
(b) Adjust for seasonal factors.
(c) Prepare a graph, and project it for the coming year 19-4.
(d) What are your quarterly forecast sales, unadjusted for seasonal variations, for the year 19-4?

10. Budgetary Control: Its Uses and Limitations

Budgeting is a useful management technique which can aid in the future guidance of a business. In today's highly competitive climate, management must strive to guide a business to a profitable position. The future is, to a large extent, uncertain. Any foresight that can be obtained will be of great benefit. A budget is, therefore, an attempt to look at the future to see what conditions will be like; to estimate what sales can reasonably be expected, and with that basic knowledge to plan the production needed for those sales; to decide what other costs and expenses will be incurred by the business, and what the net profit will be; and to estimate also the need for cash resources, the level of stocks required, the amount of credit to be given to customers, and taken from suppliers, and the need for capital investment in new equipment, vehicles or buildings. The overall equation that results may not present a satisfactory state of affairs. There may be too little profit indicated. The cash needed may be too great. The expected profit may give too poor a return on the capital invested in the business.

In sorting out these problems, and striving for a more acceptable equation, management will obtain a deep insight into the business. The weak points of the organisation will be apparent, and action can be taken to strengthen them. When the budget is finally completed it should be a well reasoned model of how the business will perform in the coming year.

The future will always be unsure, and the deeper into the future that one looks, the more uncertain it becomes. Still some indication of future happenings is always useful. Many businesses budget in brief detail for a period of five years, and then each year prepare a detailed budget for the coming year, while pushing the boundary of the five year plan another year into the future.

In order to make a budget effective, it *must* be a joint effort by the whole management team. Any attempt to impose a budget from above will result in a lack of co-operation from those actively concerned with company performance. Similarly if budgeting becomes an exercise carried out by the management accountant alone, it will not be accepted wholeheartedly by those members of the organisation who are in a position to control costs. The sales manager, failing to meet his budgeted order intake, will shelter behind the excuse that he is expected to meet unreasonable figures, in the preparation of which he had no part. The works manager, taken to task because his material and labour usage has exceeded budget, will similarly claim that the budget is unreasonable. If they have been involved in the preparation of the figures, they will be more likely to accept them as attainable.

Limiting Factors

In every budget there is a limiting factor around which it should be constructed. This factor will vary from budget to budget. It may, for example, be sales or order intake. There may be only a limited share of the market available for the products that are being manufactured. If this is so, the budget must be calculated accordingly. It would be folly to manufacture goods well in excess of customer requirement. The only result would be excessive stocks and consequent cash shortage. The budget should be reduced in line with the expected sales. If the resulting profit figure is not acceptable, further attempts should be made to squeeze more orders from customers, or place a stricter control on costs.

Another limiting factor could be productive capacity. There is a degree of flexibility in a manufacturing organisation. A single shift, with overtime, can be extended to double or treble shift working, usually without overtime, or even the continental system of continuous production throughout the seven days of every week. Each represents a means of increasing production, and only when all such possibilities in the existing buildings have been exhausted, should any attempt be made to acquire other buildings. Obviously, an increasing number of shifts may not be possible if there are problems in finding enough employees to staff them. There could also be social problems where the process is noisy, and the proximity of houses prevents night-time working. When the maximum production that can be achieved in the circumstances has been reached, it would be pointless to take further orders that could not be produced. Sales, and with it the size of the budget will, in this case, be limited by productive capacity. Other factors limiting the size of the budget are shortage of materials, shortage of skilled labour, inadequate machinery, and limited financial resources. Whatever the limiting factor, it will have the same effect of restricting the size of the budget.

Preparation of a Budget

The actual preparation of the budget will be placed in the hands of a budget co-ordinator, who will often be the management accountant. Several months before the end of the financial year he will call a meeting of all departmental heads, and they will begin working on their expected needs for the following year. Obviously there will be great pressure placed on the sales manager to supply estimates of the numbers of items that he considers can be sold, together with an indication of the probable selling price. A time-table for the supply of information will be drawn up, and this must be strictly adhered to.

When the sales information is available it can be split down into machine hours and raw material needed, and subsidiary budgets can then be prepared for such items as raw materials, production, labour, variable overheads, and fixed assets. Fixed overheads will also be estimated. When monthly turnover and purchases are known, budgets can be prepared for debtors, creditors and cash.

When all budgets have been prepared they will be used to construct an operating statement and balance sheet for the whole year, and at monthly stages throughout that year. Senior management will decide whether the overall position represents an acceptable situation, bearing in mind the capital invested, or to be invested, in the business, and the need to give an adequate return to the shareholders. Various suggestions will be made which require adjustments to the budget figures. The adjustments must, however, be realistic, and based on a solid foundation of fact. The final act, following revision, will be the adoption of the budget by the board of the company. It will then form part of company policy for the coming year.

Budgets as a Means of Control

Budgeting will give rise to the following advantages.

(1) *Annual Review* Much effort will have gone into the preparation of the budget, and many officials of the company will have achieved a greater insight into the workings of the business than they possessed before. In some progressive companies the task is being taken so seriously that a method has been evolved known as zero budgeting. Instead of basing the coming year's budget upon past experience, and adjusting for future expected happenings, a new start is made each year with a return to a zero base, and the needs of the business are built up anew. This has the great advantage that inefficiencies are not built into the system and lost sight of from year to year. Every aspect of the business then comes under a close and searching annual scrutiny, aimed at maximising efficiency.

(2) *Method of Guidance* The budget will provide management with a means of guidance through the future. A sound attempt will have been made to think about the future, to see where the company expects to be in a year's time, and how it expects to arrive there. During the course of the year, as actual results become available, they can be compared with the forecast results. Any differences must be explained, and action taken to get the company back on course, if results start to fall below the budgeted level.

(3) *Cost Control* If members of the management team have been involved in the preparation of budgets, they can be given responsibility for ensuring that budgeted costs and expenses are not exceeded in their departments. If the budget figures have been imposed from above, their effectiveness as a means of cost control, is much reduced.

(4) *Greater Co-operation* If all departments of a business have co-operated in the preparation of a budget plan, and agreed to its final form, many areas of conflict will have been eliminated. This must lead to smoother working in the organisation. Employees will see more clearly where they slot into the overall business.

(5) *Financial Thinking* Many non-financial employees think of their job only in terms of the units with which they are dealing. A salesperson thinks only of the value of order intake; a production person in terms of the numbers of units produced; a transport person in terms of the numbers of miles travelled on a journey. After

participating in a budget exercise, they will begin to think in terms of costs, and the effect of each action upon the profitability of the business. All will then be talking a common language.

Disadvantages

There are, however, some disadvantages emerging from the budgeting procedure.

(1) *Inflexibility* If the domination of budgeted figures becomes too great, there will be a reluctance to exceed budget under any circumstances. An unexpected order could arise, needing a trip abroad to clinch it. A manager too dominated by budgeted figures, who was overspent on travel, might be tempted to veto the trip, thereby losing the order. It is important, therefore, to use an intelligent approach to budgeting, and be prepared to exceed budgeted expenditure where benefit can be gained.

(2) *Divergence from Actual Figures* Where actual results differ quite considerably from budget, its effectiveness as a method of control is lost. Comparison between figures becomes meaningless. To overcome this problem it is necessary to resort to flexible budgeting. Variable costs are then increased or decreased in line with actual production, thereby restoring an effective means of control.

(3) *Imposed Figures* Where budgets are imposed from above on reluctant managers, bad feeling can result, especially if the budget is used as an excuse to browbeat those failing to achieve their targets. To overcome this, the co-operation of the managers must be won. Initially any failure to achieve budget must not be treated with undue harshness. When co-operation has been achieved, the benefits of budgeting should become apparent to all.

Assignments

10.1. You have been appointed budget accountant, with the task of co-ordinating the preparation of the annual budget. It is now June, and your budget period starts on 1st January next.
(*a*) Who will you include in your budget team?
(*b*) Draw up a timetable for the completion of the various subsidiary and master budgets.

90 Accounting for Management

10.2. Your company is considering the establishment of budgeting as a management aid. Draft a report to the managing director, advising on the usefulness, or otherwise, of such a system.

10.3. You are production manager, and your budget for overtime working has already been exceeded for the month. You are then asked to sanction overtime working on four separate occasions.
(*a*) To complete a first order for a new, major customer. The order has to be despatched on the following day.
(*b*) To complete an export order which is due to meet a boat sailing from Liverpool in three days' time. There is a penalty clause in the contract for failure to ship on time.
(*c*) To work on a job which has always been manufactured during overtime whenever it has been made.
(*d*) To work on an order which is being made for stock.
Give reasons for your decision in each case.

10.4. You occupy a small factory on the edge of an industrial estate, adjacent to a row of houses. Your production process is quite noisy. At present you work on a single shift basis, but there has been a vast and continuing increase in market demand for your product. Your machinery is modern, but there is no room for any more in your premises. Raw materials are in plentiful supply, and there is a local pool of suitable labour. You do not have sufficient finance to move into larger premises.
(*a*) What is the limiting factor in your business?
(*b*) How can you overcome it?
(*c*) If you were sited in the middle of the industrial estate, would your solution be different?

11. The Preparation of Budgets

The first stage in budgeting is to gauge the sales level that will be achieved during the budget period. The various methods indicated in Chapter 9 can be used to estimate this. There is no logic in budgeting for any other department until the sales budget is known. The various subsidiary budgets can then be prepared.

Subsidiary Budgets

At this stage a note of caution must be sounded. In practice some budgets will be almost impossible to guess accurately. Customers, for example, are very prone to change their minds. Orders can be cancelled, or additional orders placed, with very little prior warning. Some customers will not pay their accounts on time, but will try to take an extra period of credit. Production can vary because of absenteeism, industrial disputes, and a host of other reasons. In theoretical budgeting, however, it is always assumed that everything will happen according to plan. If debts are due to be paid by a certain date, they will be so paid.

In practice, budget periods will normally be of twelve months duration, analysed into monthly sub-sections, corresponding to the normal monthly accounting periods. To save time, budget periods of six months are used in this book.

A budget period will carry on from the final accounts of the current period. A Wright Co. Ltd has prepared accounts for the year to 31st December 19-9, and it is required to budget for the six-month period to 30th June 19-0. The balance sheet at 31st December 19-9 was:

A. Wright Co. Ltd
Balance Sheet at 31st December 19-9

			£
Issued share capital (£1 Ordinary Shares)			350 000
Reserves			129 600
Capital employed			£479 600

Represented by:			£
Fixed assets:	Cost	Depreciation	
	£	£	
Machinery	220 000	104 000	116 000
Vehicles	35 000	18 000	17 000
	255 000	122 000	133 000

Current assets:

Stock of raw materials		36 000
Finished goods (2 400 units)		21 600
		57 600
Debtors		
(Oct. £117 000,		
Nov. £130 000 &		
Dec. £128 000)		375 000
Cash at bank		18 000
		450 600

Less Current liabilities:

Creditors for materials	59 000		
Creditors for variable overheads	9 000		
Creditors for fixed overheads	36 000	104 000	346 600
			£479 600

The following information has been collected for the budget period:
(1) Sales at £20 per unit:

The Preparation of Budgets

	January	February	March	April	May	June
Units	4 300	6 200	8 100	4 200	7 100	8 100

(2) Production is to be as stable as possible throughout the period, with a closing stock in June of 3 400 units.

(3) Unit production costs are expected to be:

	£
Raw materials	5
Direct labour	3
Variable overheads	2
	10

(4) Monthly purchases of raw materials should be:

January	February	March	April	May	June
£	£	£	£	£	£
34 000	30 000	29 000	37 000	34 000	32 000

(5) Customers pay their accounts during the third month after the month of sale.

(6) Creditors for materials are paid during the second month after purchase.

(7) Variable overheads are paid on the basis of 25% in the month of production, and 75% in the month following.

(8) Fixed overheads of £40 000 per month are paid during the following month.

(9) Three automatic lathes are purchased for £75 000, and paid for in April.

(10) Depreciation on machinery will be £3 000 per month until March, increasing to £4 000 per month for the rest of the period. Depreciation on vehicles will be £500 per month.

(11) Wages are paid during the month of production.

With this information it is possible to start constructing the budget.

(a) Sales Budget

As it is known that sales will be made at £20 per unit, the value of monthly sales during the period will be calculated by multiplying the units sold each month by £20. The budget will be:

January	February	March	April	May	June	Total
£	£	£	£	£	£	£
86 000	124 000	162 000	84 000	142 000	162 000	760 000

It is then possible to proceed to the next stage.

(b) Production Budget (in units)

When an order is received from a customer it is expected to be delivered on time. The customers' requirements, however, may be erratic. Some months may require deliveries far in excess of normal production capacity. Other months may be well below capacity. The problem may be overcome by spreading production evenly over the year. Such a policy makes sound sense, as it maintains an even production demand upon the works throughout the year. This eliminates the need for alternative periods of shorttime and overtime working, both of which are inefficient.

An even level of production can be calculated from the sales budget if the required stock levels are also known. The opening stock on 1st January is known to be 2 400 units, and the closing stock on 30th June is required to be 3 400 units. The production required will be:

Monthly sales for the six months	38 000
Add Stock increase over the period	1 000
Required production	39 000

Each month's production must be $\dfrac{39\,000}{6} = 6\,500$ units.

The production budget in units will be:

	January	February	March	April	May	June
Opening stock	2 400	4 600	4 900	3 300	5 600	5 000
Add Production	6 500	6 500	6 500	6 500	6 500	6 500
	8 900	11 100	11 400	9 800	12 100	11 500
Less Sales	4 300	6 200	8 100	4 200	7 100	8 100
Closing stock	4 600	4 900	3 300	5 600	5 000	3 400

There might be a further constraint that stock should never fall below a minimum of 3 400 units, with any necessary increase in production being carried out in January. In this case the difference between 3 400 and the lowest stock revealed in March of 3 300, or 100 extra units, will be produced in January. This will increase stocks all through by 100, and the final stock will be 3 500 units.

It must be noted that high stocks require to be financed, and this must have an effect on the cash budget.

(c) *Raw Materials Budget*

As monthly production is now known, it will be possible to check that monthly material purchases are adequate. Unless there are special circumstances, such as shortages, or special terms for bulk buying, purchases should be roughly in line with production. Allowance should be made for the length of the production cycle — the time taken to manufacture the product from raw material to finished stage. The opening balance sheet records the stock of raw materials at £36 000. Monthly purchases are known, and the material content of each unit of production is £5. The materials budget can now be prepared.

	January	February	March	April	May	June
	£	£	£	£	£	£
Opening stock	36 000	37 500	35 000	31 500	36 000	37 500
Add Purchases	34 000	30 000	29 000	37 000	34 000	32 000
	70 000	67 500	64 000	68 500	70 000	69 500
Less Usage	32 500	32 500	32 500	32 500	32 500	32 500
Closing stock	£37 500	£35 000	£31 500	£36 000	£37 500	£37 000

This seems reasonable, with no violent stock fluctuations.

(d) *Production Budget (in value)*

Working from the production budget in units, we can calculate the number of direct employees required to provide the labour budget. The level of variable overheads can be calculated from the quantities of units that will be produced.

The costs of production can be computed by evaluating production by the estimated unit cost of raw materials, direct labour and variable overheads. These are known to be:

	£
Direct materials	5
Direct labour	3
Variable overheads	2
	10

The budget will be:

	January £	February £	March £	April £	May £	June £	Total £
Direct materials	32 500	32 500	32 500	32 500	32 500	32 500	195 000
Direct labour	19 500	19 500	19 500	19 500	19 500	19 500	117 000
Variable overheads	13 000	13 000	13 000	13 000	13 000	13 000	78 000
	£65 000	£65 000	£65 000	£65 000	£65 000	£65 000	£390 000

(e) *Fixed Overheads Budget*

Fixed overheads will not vary with production, but will remain as a static charge. If during the budget period there is an increase in an element of cost — say extra administrative staff being recruited, or an increase in rent or rates part of the way through the period — there will be a corresponding increase in budgeted fixed overheads. Apart from this, it will be normal to have fixed overheads spread equally throughout the period, giving the same charge in accounting periods of similar length. The monthly charge in the example is estimated at £40 000.

(f) *Debtors Budget*

The length of time taken by customers to pay their accounts can have a major influence upon cash flow in a business. A decision is made on the credit policy to be adopted — and strictly adhered to — and it can then be seen how much capital will be tied up in financing debtors.

Sales are made at £20 per unit, and customers pay during the third month after the month of sale. The first three months of the budget period will expect to receive payment for the sales of October, November and December of the previous year. These were respectively £117 000, £130 000 and £128 000. The budget will appear as follows.

	January £	February £	March £	April £	May £	June £
Opening balances	375 000	344 000	338 000	372 000	370 000	388 000
Add Sales	86 000	124 000	162 000	84 000	142 000	162 000
	461 000	468 000	500 000	456 000	512 000	550 000
Less Cash received	117 000	130 000	128 000	86 000	124 000	162 000
Closing balances	£344 000	£338 000	£372 000	£370 000	£388 000	£388 000

If the calculation is correct the closing balance should equal the sales of the period March to June, or £84 000, £142 000 and £162 000, which equal £388 000.

(g) *Creditors for Materials Budget*

Extended credit taken from suppliers can be a useful means of financing a business. Having decided upon the credit period allowed by suppliers, the creditors budget can be constructed. The principles are similar to those adopted in the debtors budget. Suppliers are paid during the second month after purchase. Thus November's purchases of £26 000 will be paid for during January, and December's purchases of £33 000 during February. Following the same format as the debtors budget, the creditors budget will be:

	January £	February £	March £	April £	May £	June £
Opening balances	59 000	67 000	64 000	59 000	66 000	71 000
Add Purchases	34 000	30 000	29 000	37 000	34 000	32 000
	93 000	97 000	93 000	96 000	100 000	103 000
Less Payments	26 000	33 000	34 000	30 000	29 000	37 000
Closing balances	£67 000	£64 000	£59 000	£66 000	£71 000	£66 000

As with the debtors budget, the accuracy of the final balance can be checked. It should equal the purchases of May and June, namely £34 000 and £32 000, which equal £66 000.

(h) Capital Budget

This budget will be concerned with estimating the expenditure on fixed assets. Any investment here will reduce the amount of cash available to pay normal trade creditors, and finance stock and debtors. Large items of equipment often require prompt payment, so limited credit is available. During the budget period three new automatic lathes are to be purchased in April for £75 000, payment to be made on delivery.

Allied to this budget will be a calculation of depreciation to be charged. This should be the same for all equal length accounting periods, only altering when there is a purchase or sale of an asset, as happens in April. Budgeted depreciation will be:

	January £	February £	March £	April £	May £	June £	Total £
Machinery	3 000	3 000	3 000	4 000	4 000	4 000	21 000
Vehicles	500	500	500	500	500	500	3 000
	£3 500	£3 500	£3 500	£4 500	£4 500	£4 500	£24 000

(j) Cash Budget

The cash budget is one of the most valuable budgets. It is, of course, important to know whether a business is making a profit or loss. Despite this, many a fine business has run into serious problems because of a shortage of cash, although it has been making adequate profits. Cash shortages can result from:

(i)   Excessive investment in fixed assets.
(ii) Excessive stock-holding.
(iii) Allowing too much credit to customers.
(iv) Paying suppliers too quickly.
(v)   Making losses over a long period.

Cash flow acts in a strange way. When a business enters a period of lower trading, the immediate result is an improvement in cash flow. This is due to lower expenditure on stock and labour, while debtors are being collected from a period when sales were higher. Thereafter, this temporary surplus of cash rapidly disappears if losses are being made. When an upturn in trade takes place, and more labour needs to be hired, and greater stocks need to be held to support higher production, a cash famine strikes.

There are means of alleviating the position, either by introducing permanent, long-term capital, or the more temporary expedient of borrowing from a bank to cover short-term cash shortages. The bank manager will not look with favour upon a customer who seeks an immediate loan because unforeseen events have cropped up, and there is no cash to pay this week's wages. Far greater consideration is given to the customer who knows, months in advance, that cash shortages are likely to arise. That customer is the one who prepares cash budgets, either in isolation, or as part of an overall system of budgeting.

Generally, budgets are used as a means of estimating profit. Budgeted figures are included on the basis of when expenses are incurred. In the case of a cash budget, this is not so. It is necessary to know not when a sale or purchase is made, but when it is paid for. This means offsetting figures used in other budgets.

Much information about payment dates is already known, and from the opening balance sheet information is known about outstanding debtors and creditors. The best method of computing the budget is to calculate receipts first, then payments, and finally put it all together in the budget format.

	January £	February £	March £	April £	May £	June £
Receipts:						
Sales	£117 000	£130 000	£128 000	£86 000	£124 000	£162 000

	January £	February £	March £	April £	May £	June £
Payments						
Materials	26 000	33 000	34 000	30 000	29 000	37 000
Labour	19 500	19 500	19 500	19 500	19 500	19 500
Variable						
overheads 25%	3 250	3 250	3 250	3 250	3 250	3 250
75%	9 000	9 750	9 750	9 750	9 750	9 750
Fixed						
overheads	36 000	40 000	40 000	40 000	40 000	40 000
Machinery	—	—	—	75 000	—	—
	£93 750	£105 500	£106 500	£177 500	£101 500	£109 500

Cash Budget

	January	February	March	April	May	June
Opening balance	18 000	41 250	65 750	87 250	(4 250)	18 250
Add Receipts	117 000	130 000	128 000	86 000	124 000	162 000
	135 000	171 250	193 750	173 250	119 750	180 250
Less Payments	93 750	105 500	106 500	177 500	101 500	109 500
	£41 250	£65 750	£87 250	£(4 250)	£18 250	£70 750

The cash balance at the end of the period shows a healthy increase over that at the beginning, despite the investment in new machinery. The wisdom of preparing the budget is shown, however, by the overdrawn position shown at the end of April. Although it is only a small overdraft, which disappears the next month, it is an ideal situation for a bank overdraft. The position is known well in advance, and will be cleared in a very short time. In practice, the problem could well be overcome by holding back some payments of creditors until the next month.

(k) Master Budget

Having prepared the subsidiary budgets, it is now possible to pick up the various items of information required to prepare the master budget. This is an operating statement covering both trading and profit and loss accounts, and an estimated balance sheet at the end of the accounting period.

Operating Statement for the period 1st January to 30th June 19-0

		£	£
Sales			760 000
Less	Cost of sales:		
	Opening stock	21 600	
Add	Production	390 000	
		411 600	
Less	Closing stock (3 400 × £10)	34 000	377 600
Gross profit			382 400
Less	Fixed overheads (6 × £40 000)	240 000	
Depreciation		24 000	264 000
Net profit			£118 400

Estimated Balance Sheet at 30th June 19-0

	£	£	£
Issued share capital			
(£1 ordinary shares)			350 000
Reserves			
(£129 600 + £118 400)			248 000
Capital employed			£598 000

	£	£	£
Represented by:			
Fixed assets:			
	Cost	Depreciation	
Machinery	295 000	125 000	170 000
Vehicles	35 000	21 000	14 000
	330 00	146 000	184 000

Current assets:			
Stock			
(Raw materials £37 000;			
Finished goods £34 000)		71 000	
Debtors		388 000	
Cash at bank		70 750	
		529 750	
Less Current liabilities:			
Creditors for materials	66 000		
Creditors for variable overheads	9 750		
Creditors for fixed overheads	40 000	115 750	414 000
			£598 000

Departmental Budgets

Having completed the master budget for the whole organisation, the next step is to break it down between the various departments of the business. In many cases this will not be necessary, if budgeting has been carried out with the active participation of departmental heads. They will have supplied the information that has been incorporated in the master budget. There may, in some circumstances, be information incorporated in the budget that has been obtained outside the department, and will have to be allocated on a logical basis. An example of this would be depreciation on fixed assets. The person responsible for maintaining depreciation records is normally the management accountant.

In many cases there will be little difficulty in allocating the costs to departments. Labour costs will be charged to the departments where the employees are working. Materials will be charged to the departments in which they are issued to production. Some overheads will be equally easy to allocate, such as indirect labour to the department in which the employee is working. Others will be less easy, and must be allocated on an arbitrary but logical basis. Rent and rates could be allocated upon the basis of floor area; heating and lighting on the cubic capacity of each department.

When all costs have been allocated to the departments of the business, it will be possible to analyse each month's actual results on the same basis, and compare them with the departmental budget figures. This is a useful method of control. The departmental manager can be held responsible for the costs of his department, to ensure that, as far as is possible, actual cost does not exceed budget during the year.

Assignments

11.1. P. Daley Ltd. commenced business on 1st July, 19-9
The proposals and estimates for the next three months to 30th September 19-9 are as follows:
- (a) The Company will issue 15 000 £1 ordinary shares payable in full on 1st July 19-9.
- (b) Fixtures and fittings costing £4 000 will be obtained and paid for on 1st July; depreciation is to be provided at the rate of 10% per annum on cost.
- (c) Five delivery vans costing £3 000 each are to be obtained on 1st July, for which a deposit of £400 cash on each is required. The balance is to be paid in eight equal monthly instalments commencing on 31st July 19-9. The vans are to be depreciated at the rate of 20% per annum on cost. Ignore interest on hire purchase.
- (d) An initial stock of goods is to be bought on 1st July at a cost of £22 500 (£3 per unit) and subsequent purchases at £3 per unit are to be made so that this stock level is maintained at the end of each month. Suppliers are paid during the month following that of purchase.
- (e) All sales are on credit at the uniform rate of £5 per unit, and the estimates are:

    | July | 6 000 units |
    | August | 7 000 units |
    | September | 8 000 units |

    Debtors will pay in the second month after the month of sale.

(f) Administration expenses are expected to be 20% of sales and are paid during the month in which they are incurred.

REQUIRED:

(a) A cash budget for the three months ended 30th September 19-9, assuming that the bank will agree to any overdraft that becomes necessary.
(b) A projected Trading and Profit and Loss Account for the three months ending 30th September 19-9.
(c) A projected Balance Sheet at 30th September 19-9.

11.2. On the first Monday morning of every month the sales manager and works manager of a manufacturing company meet to plan future production in the light of customers' orders. At the beginning of April 19-4 the firm orders for the next six months, in units, were:

April	27 000
May	24 600
June	29 300
July	30 400
August	26 300
September	35 000

Stocks of finished items at 31st March were 3 600. It was decided that the stock should be increased to 5 000 units as soon as possible, and should be maintained at that level. Normal monthly production is 28 000 units. Overtime working can increase production by a maximum of 10%. Each month contains 4 weeks.

It was decided to work overtime immediately, in order to build up sufficient stocks to cope for the remainder of the period with normal working.

In which week will overtime cease?

11.3. John Smith won £2 000 on the football pools, and decided to establish his own business. His winnings were paid into a bank current account on 1st January 19-3, and he anticipated that his receipts and payments until 30th June would be as follows:

(a) On 1st January a second-hand van will be purchased for £4 000. A deposit of £1 000 is payable immediately, with the balance in three equal instalments payable on the first day of each subsequent month.

(b) Stock purchases at £2 per unit will be:

January	February	March	April	May	June
2 000	3 000	4 500	5 000	6 500	4 000

Creditors are to be paid in the second month after the date of purchase.

(c) Monthly sales in units at £3 per unit will be:

January	February	March	April	May	June
1 000	1 900	3 100	4 800	5 700	6 500

Payment is expected to be made on the basis of one third in the month of sale, with the balance in the following month.

(d) Wages and salaries, payable at the end of each month, will be £1 500 per month.

(e) Drawings will be: March £400; May £700; June £300.

(f) A commission will be paid to an agent at the rate of 1% of sales, payable in the month following the sale.

(g) General variable expenses are 3% of sales, and fixed expenses are £200 per month, both being paid in the actual month.

REQUIRED:

Prepare a monthly cash budget for the first six months of trading.

11.4. The balance sheet of Jack Black at 31st December 19-1 was:

Fixed assets:	£	£
Machinery		30 000
Fixtures		10 000
Vehicles		8 000
		48 000
Current assets:		
Stock — Raw materials	4 000	
— Finished goods (1 500 units)	6 000	

	£	£
Debtors — (Oct. £8 000, Nov. £11 000, Dec. £9 000)	28 000	
Bank	900	
	38 900	
Less Current liabilities:		
Creditors for materials (Nov. £10 000, Dec. £8 000)	18 000	
Creditors for variable overheads	2 000	
Creditors for fixed overheads	2 000	
	22 000	
		16 900
		64 900

Financed by:	£
Capital Account	64 900

The following information has been collected for budget purposes:
(1) Sales for the period at £7 per unit are expected to be:

January	February	March	April	May	June
2 000	2 500	3 000	3 000	3 500	3 000

Customers pay their accounts in the third month after sale.
(2) Unit production costs are expected to be stable throughout the period at:

Raw material	£2
Direct labour	£1
Variable overheads	£1

Production is to be evenly maintained throughout the period, with finished stock being raised to 2 500 units.
(3) Monthly purchases of raw materials will be:

January	February	March	April	May	June
£	£	£	£	£	£
5 000	5 000	7 000	7 000	8 000	8 000

Payment is to be made in the second month after purchase.

(4) Wages are paid during the month of production.
(5) Variable overheads are paid on the basis of 20% during the month of production, and 80% in the following month.
(6) Fixed overheads are paid after one month, at the rate of £2 200 per month.
(7) Depreciate fixed assets on the following bases:

Machinery	15% per annum on book value.
Fixtures	10% per annum on book value.
Vehicles	25% per annum on book values.

(8) New machinery costing £6 000 is to be installed on 1st April, and will be paid for in six equal monthly instalments, commencing on that day. Ignore interest charges.

REQUIRED:

(a) Prepare all the necessary subsidiary budgets, together with a projected Operating Account for the six months to 30th June 19-2, and an estimated Balance Sheet at that date.

(b) Would you recommend any special action on the part of the owner?

Part III
Analysis and Interpretation of Accounting Information

12. Capital

At an early stage in the study of accountancy the word 'capital' is mentioned. Take the case of a person who has amassed some savings, and decides to set up in business on his, or her, own account. The savings are introduced into the business in the form of cash. The first book-keeping entry is to debit the cash book and post to the credit of the owner's capital account. The money forming the assets of the business represents the full amount that the business now owes to its owner. In other words, capital represents the value that has been introduced into it by its owner(s) in order that the business may be carried on. This holds true in the case of a sole trader; a partnership where several people introduce capital into a business; and a limited company where many individuals, through the buying of shares, provide the capital which enables the business to be carried on.

If £500 000 of ordinary share capital is issued by a new company the initial balance sheet will be:

	£		£
Issued Ordinary shares of £1	500 000	Cash at bank	500 000

The cash introduced with the object of starting a business does not remain in that form for long. Premises are required, which may be rented or bought. Money is paid out for a building, or the right to occupy a building for a period of time where rent is paid. Where a building is bought, the decline in cash assets will be offset by the asset of buildings owned. Machinery for manufacture will be bought. Fixtures and fittings and motor vehicles will also be needed. Where these are purchased for cash their acquisition will offset the fall in cash resources. At the end of this spending spree the business will have the fixed assets which will enable it to carry on its chosen activity. The capital, however, will still be the same, but instead of being represented by cash alone, it will now be represented by buildings, machinery, fixtures and fittings, motor vehicles and cash.

The cash that has been used to purchase the various fixed assets will not return as cash for many years, and when it does, will be very much reduced in value. The fixed assets are needed to enable the business to be carried on, and in most cases will fall in value over the years. When the assets are finally sold, they will often fetch little more than scrap value. The only exception will be buildings, which tend to increase in value over a period of many decades. The result as far as the business is concerned, is that the money invested in these fixed assets will have gone out of circulation. At this stage the business has not even commenced to manufacture or trade.

That part of the original capital that still remains as cash can now be used to purchase the necessary materials with which trading can begin. In the case of a manufacturing business, raw materials must be purchased and labour hired which can then use the machinery of the business to manufacture a finished product for sale to customers. In the case of a trading business finished goods will be bought for resale to customers. The amount of cash required to purchase stock will vary with the type of business. A manufacturing company will often only manufacture when a customer's order has been received. This reduces considerably the amount of stock that it will need to hold. A trading organisation, on the other hand, will need a much larger stock of goods to satisfy its customers who will want goods delivered quickly. If the goods are not available, the customers will go elsewhere for them.

When adequate stocks have been acquired, the capital account balance will still not have altered. It will be the same as it was when the business commenced. It will, however, now be represented by fixed assets, stock and cash. The balance sheet will be:

Balance Sheet before trading commences

	£		£	£
Issued Ordinary shares of £1	500 000	*Fixed assets*:		
		Property		200 000
		Machinery		100 000
		Fixtures and fittings		50 000
		Motor vehicles		25 000
				375 000
		Current assets:		
		Stock	50 000	
		Cash	75 000	125 000
	£500 000			£500 000

The next stage takes place when customers appear on the scene. They will buy goods available for sale, and the secret of success in business is to persuade them to pay more for the goods than they actually cost. This difference represents the *gross margin*, or *gross profit*.

Customers may pay for the goods in two different ways:

(*a*) *Cash Sales* This means that they pay cash at the point of sale. In effect the business exchanges the goods for cash. The cash is then immediately available to buy more stock or pay for the expenses of running the business.

(*b*) *Credit Sales* This is the more usual method of conducting business. The goods change hands, and payment will be made at some time in the future — usually at the end of the month following the month of sale. During the waiting period, the amount owing by customers is known as *debtors*. These debtors are another form of asset, and will represent a part of the capital of the business.

Apart from the fixed assets the capital will now also be represented by three other assets:

(i) Stock.
(ii) Debtors.
(iii) Cash at bank and in hand.

These three assets are collectively known as *current assets*. Like the current in a stream they are continually moving — cash becomes stock, which in turn is sold to become debtors, and finally, as the debtors pay, cash once more is received. The cycle then recommences with the purchase of more stock.

As trading has now commenced, it may be assumed that profit will have been made. Gross profit will arise at the point of sale, when customers are persuaded to pay more for goods than they have cost. Out of the gross profit the expenses of the business will be paid. Any balance remaining will be net profit. This belongs to the owners of the business, and will represent a reserve. In effect it becomes additional capital. It will be represented by several assets. As gross profit is realised into cash when the debtors pay, part is swallowed up by the expenses of running the business. The net profit remaining then gets converted into stock or further debtors. It might be tied up also in additional fixed asset investment. Assuming that £50 000 net profit has now been made, the balance sheet might now appear as follows.

Balance Sheet after the Commencement of Trading

	£		£	£
Issued Ordinary shares of £1	500 000	Fixed Assets (as before)		375 000
Reserves:		Current Assets		
Profit and Loss	50 000	Stock	60 000	
		Debtors	80 000	
		Cash	35 000	175 000
	£550 000			£550 000

We have so far seen a business in which all purchases have been for cash, and the sole source of finance has been issued share capital and retained profit. The size of the business will be restricted by the amount of capital introduced, and expansion will be dependent upon further capital being invested. The cheapest and easiest method of doing this is to purchase goods on credit. When a supplier is delivering goods for which payment will not be made for approximately six to eight weeks, the effect is just the same as an injection of fresh capital of an equivalent amount. The goods will become stock, and some of the stock may even be sold and converted into debtors, before payment needs to be made. It is, moreover, often possible to take extra credit from suppliers, thus increasing the size of the capital injection into the firm. It must also be remembered that the firm's customers will be doing the same thing, and care must be taken that excessive debtors are not allowed to accumulate. If they do build up, extra capital will be needed to finance them.

The result of an extra injection of capital from suppliers will be to:

(*a*) Make more stock available.
(*b*) Possibly allow more machinery to be acquired.
(*c*) Enable a larger volume of debtors, resulting from a higher turnover, to be financed.

With increased turnover higher profit should result (say £70 000 as opposed to £50 000) and the balance sheet could appear as follows:

Balance Sheet affected by credit purchases

	£		£	£
Issued Ordinary Shares of £1	500 000	*Fixed assets* (as before)		375 000
Reserves:		*Current assets*:		
Profit & Loss	70 000	Stock	70 000	
		Debtors	120 000	
Current liabilities:		Cash	45 000	235 000
Creditors	40 000			
	£610 000			£610 000

Working Capital

The bottom half of the balance sheet now provides enough information to calculate the working capital of the business. It may be defined as the capital required for the day to day running of the business — the purchasing and holding of stocks, the financing of debtors and the maintenance of a sufficient cash balance to meet immediate payments. This will be offset by the amount of credit given by suppliers of goods and services, known collectively as creditors.

The control of working capital is a vital function of business management. Another description is net current assets, and this adequately describes the true nature of these assets. They are moving all the time, rising and falling daily. There is no comparison with fixed assets. Once a decision has been made to invest in new fixed assets, and the investment has been made, more fixed capital will not be needed until a further positive decision is made to increase investment. Such is not the case with current assets. From their very nature these assets are constantly moving. New stock is being bought — and it is fatally easy to overstock. Excessive quantities may be purchased because the price appears to be 'right'. Stock is held which has become redundant due to a change in customer demand. Work in progress — the stock of part-finished goods on the shop floor — can so easily build up. Lack of a small component can hold up large orders; sickness amongst the labour force can cause jobs to be held up between processes; poor production control, whereby urgent jobs are constantly introduced before larger orders have been finished, can result in production bottlenecks. Finally finished stock can build up. When orders are low, stock orders can be manufactured to keep the labour force employed. These will be products of a standardised nature, which normally sell to a wide range of customers. There is an excellent possibility that orders for them will ultimately be received. If, however, their receipt is long delayed, finished stock can expand to alarming proportions.

The main danger is that production can only take place with labour that has been paid, and materials that have been paid for, or will shortly be paid for. This requires cash. If stocks get too high there could be insufficient cash available to pay creditors, or the wages of the workforce.

Look also at the position of debtors. The stock that has been sold to them will probably already have been paid for, thus using up valuable cash resources. The sales of this business will represent purchases to its customers who will realise the virtue of financing their businesses by taking extended credit from their suppliers. Unless constant vigilance is exercised, debtors will rise, thus tying up more capital, and reducing cash resources. If sales are increasing, it will be even more important to control debtors, which will be automatically increased as sales rise. If customers pay regularly two full months after the month of sale, there will be three full months of sales outstanding at any time. If sales are running at £40 000 per month, debtors will be £120 000. If, however, sales are averaging £60 000 per month, debtors will be £180 000. Thus greater working capital will be required to finance higher sales.

Action can be taken to minimise the amount of working capital tied up as working capital:

(*a*) Stock can be strictly controlled by buying only limited amounts of materials; seeing that work in progress stock does not build up on the shop floor; and limiting the amount of finished stock held, in line with anticipated sales.

(b) Debtors can be reduced by an efficient method of credit control. This involves reminding customers when debts are due for payment, threatening obdurate customers, and even taking stubborn payers to court. Credit control must be used in an intelligent manner, as indiscriminate browbeating can alienate customers altogether.

(c) Greater credit can be taken from suppliers, up to a limit. If too much credit is taken, the goodwill of the supplier is alienated, and this can lead to threats, and the commencement of legal proceedings. If judgment is obtained by a supplier, the fact is rapidly noted by all credit agencies, and this can cause great difficulties in obtaining credit from new suppliers in the future.

(d) Bank overdraft facilities can be arranged. A bank manager is rarely interested in providing long-term finance for a business, but will often be delighted to provide short-term finance, especially for a soundly run business. Collateral security must be available. The bank manager will take a floating charge over the assets of the business. If at any time the overdraft cannot be repaid, he then has the right to take over the business, and sell the assets to recover the debt due to him. In small businesses, where the assets are insufficient to cover an overdraft, similar rights will be taken over the personal assets of the directors who are also shareholders. An overdraft is a facility granted by a bank, whereby a customer can spend more than he has in his account, up to a limit fixed by the manager. Interest is charged on the loan on a daily basis. The bank thus provides some of the finance of working capital that would otherwise have to be provided by the owners of the business. Although overdrafts are usually granted for a period of twelve months at a time, a bank manager may demand immediate repayment of the overdraft, if he suspects that a business is getting into financial difficulties. If this cannot be done, he will exercise his right to take over and sell the assets of the business to recover the loan. An overdraft, for this reason, is treated as a current asset, and not a long-term liability.

Overall Capital Structure

The approach to the problems of financing a business depends on the nature of that business. In the case of a sole trader or partnership, capital is introduced to finance the business. Any profit that is made is distributed between the owners in their agreed profit sharing ratios, and added to the capital accounts. In the case of a limited company, the problem is more complex. The number of owners can be considerable, and they finance the business through the purchase of shares. Except in the case of relatively small companies, the ownership of the business and its management will be in different hands. Shares are purchased not as a means of obtaining employment, but mainly as a form of investment, from which an income will be expected. The running of the company is vested in the hands of a board of directors, which will be answerable to the owners or shareholders, once a year at an annual general meeting.

The directors, as custodians of the company, will recommend the payment of a dividend each year. It is rarely the full amount of available profit as, once paid, it would prove difficult to bring back if the company required further finance for expansion. The directors will, therefore, retain a portion of the profit in the company for future expansion, and then declare a dividend from the balance that is left. The retained balance then becomes a reserve. If profits are poor, the dividend will be poor. If profits are good, the dividend will be handsome — subject, of course, to government restrictive legislation. To overcome the fluctuating dividend which may arise, and to tailor it to the investor's requirements, two main categories of share are possible.

(a) Preference Shares The owners of these shares are entitled to a fixed percentage dividend whether profits are good or poor. If the dividend is not paid in any year, the right will usually cumulate to the next year. The preference shareholders have a preferential right to dividend, and no ordinary dividend can be paid if any preference dividend is in arrears. In the event of liquidation, where the company ceases to exist, the holders receive usually only the nominal value of the shares.

(b) Ordinary Shares These give the right to all the profits remaining after preference dividends have been paid, and all retained profits and surplus assets in a liquidation. This means ownership of all the

net assets of the business, apart from those required to pay the holders of loans and preference shares.

Loans

Additional finance for a business may also be raised in the form of long-term loans or debentures. This form of finance applies to sole traders and partnerships just as much as to companies. Loans will require the payment of a rate of interest, and in the case of companies, this will be fixed at the time of issue. If the loan is secured upon assets of the business, it will be called a *debenture*. As loans and debentures are not proprietors' capital, the interest payable on them is a legitimate charge in the profit and loss account of the business, and not a method of allocating profit, as in the case of dividends on shares.

These two categories, shares and loans, form the main source of capital employed in a business. Shares usually remain in existence as long as the company is in being. With loans, however, a date is fixed for repayment at some time in the future.

Reserves

The reserves of a company may arise in three different ways:

(*a*) Through the retention of profit.
(*b*) Through increase in the value of an asset.
(*c*) Through the issue of shares at more than nominal value, the difference being placed to a share premium account.

There is a major difference between share capital and reserves. Shares are not normally repaid. Once they are issued, they remain in existence for the full life of the company. Reserves, however, may theoretically be distributed to the shareholders, although in practice this is often not possible. Dividends can only be paid if there is sufficient cash available, and it has already been seen how great are the pressures upon cash in a business. In any case, that section of capital and reserves which has been invested in fixed assets can only be turned into cash by selling those assets — and that often foretells the end of a business. If shares are required in a business as long as it exists, and fixed assets are also so required, there is a strong connection between the two. The issued share capital and reserves should really be at least as great as the fixed assets, and ideally a little larger, to finance some of the working capital.

A common practice is to turn some of the reserves into shares. They are issued to existing shareholders in proportion to their shareholdings. This leaves long-term loans to finance the balance of working capital.

The assets of a company, and their finance, can be diagramatically described as in Fig. 12.1.

Capital	Assets
Issued share capital	Fixed assets
Reserves	
Long term loans	Current assets

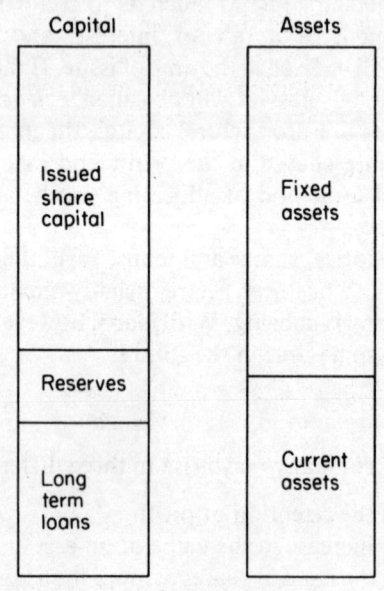

Fig. 12.1 *Financing the assets of a company*

Assignments

12.1. What are the main sources of capital, both long term and short term for:

(a) A sole trader?
(b) A partnership?
(c) A limited company?

12.2. How do fixed assets differ from current assets?

12.3. Why is it necessary for a business to have a strong credit control policy?

12.4. What is working capital? Why is its control vital to the success of a business?

12.5. You have recently purchased a considerable quantity of new equipment, which has made you very short of cash. Your creditors are pressing for payment, and you have to act quickly to obtain additional capital.

(*a*) What course of action would you recommend?
(*b*) Would your recommendation differ if the cash shortage were due to excessive stockholding?

12.6. How does the distribution of profit in the following businesses differ?

(*a*) A sole trader.
(*b*) A partnership.
(*c*) A limited company.

12.7 Write to the secretary of a local public company, and ask for a copy of the latest published accounts. Study them, and answer the following questions.

(*a*) How is the business being financed?
(*b*) Does it require to raise extra capital?
(*c*) If so, suggest the type of capital that should be considered, giving your reasons.
(*d*) Can you make a case for capitalising reserves?

12.8 You are considering the formation of a company to run a do-it-yourself shop. You have to decide:

(*a*) How much capital is required.
(*b*) What type of capital it should be.

What aspects should you consider in arriving at your decision?

13. Cash Flow and Flow of Funds

It is generally acknowledged that no business can be satisfactorily managed unless close attention is paid to its cash needs. Cash flow is the life blood of an organisation. Without it a business will cease to function. Cash is used to acquire the fixed assets without which a business cannot be carried on. It is used to purchase the stock that is either sold in the case of a trading organisation, or used to make the finished product, which is then sold, by the manufacturing organisation. The stock, when sold, becomes debtors. In due course the debts are paid in cash, thus replenishing the cash supplies. Meanwhile the business will be paying its running expenses out of its available cash.

At the point of sales gross profit is created. Whereas cash is exchanged for an equivalent amount of stock, when stock is sold its value is enhanced by gross profit, to form a higher value of debtors. As debtors pay this gross profit becomes cash, and is available to pay the expenses of the business. That portion of the gross profit not used in the running of the business, becomes available for reinvestment, either as fixed assets, or as more stock which will ultimately become debtors once more. Any shortening of the cash flow cycle by means of credit taken from suppliers, helps to reduce the amount of cash needed in the business. The crucial function of cash can be judged from the following diagram of a trading organisation.

The bank account is at the centre of the operation. It supplies cash to the whole organisation, and if the demands of any part get too great, other parts of the business will suffer. If stockholding becomes excessive, cash must be syphoned from other parts of the organisation. If that does not happen, the available cash in the

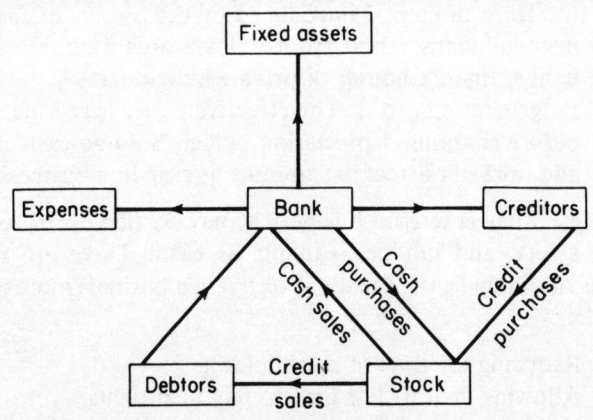

Fig. 13.1 *The flow of cash through a business*

business will decline until it reaches the point where there is insufficient cash available to meet the demands of creditors. Writs will be served for non-payment of debts, and the business will be well on the way to financial disaster.

Business transactions are based upon good faith. If credit is given by a supplier, payment is expected to be made by the due date. If it is not, and application to the courts is made, the creditworthiness of the defaulting business becomes suspect. A successfully issued writ will be recorded in the files of credit agencies. The defaulting business will then find great difficulty in obtaining credit. There are few available courses then left open to it other than the following:

(*a*) Introduce fresh capital to overcome the cash shortage.
(*b*) Contract until the business is small enough to survive on the available cash resources.
(*c*) Sell out to another business.
(*d*) Cease to exist.

Cash flow is, then, a vital aspect of every business, and management is paying increasing attention to it. At all costs there must be enough cash available to meet the demands of creditors.

Sources of Cash

There are two principal ways by which cash can enter a business.

(a) It can be introduced from an outside source. This may take the form of capital introduced by the owners of the business, or loans raised from outside organisations such as banks, finance houses or private individuals.

(b) By generating profit. The effective figure here is net profit *before* charging depreciation, which is a non-cash charge, and does not affect the amount of cash in a business.

Once cash has entered a business it may be tied up in fixed or current assets, and not be available as cash. There are several methods of making cash already invested in a business more readily available:

(a) Reducing the level of stockholding.
(b) Allowing debtors less time to pay their debts.
(c) Cutting back on fixed asset investment, or selling surplus fixed assets.
(d) Taking longer credit from suppliers.
(e) Reducing the running expenses of the business. This will also result in a higher net profit.

Applications of Cash

When cash has been introduced into a business it quickly gets deployed throughout the whole organisation, and can be tied up in several ways.

(a) *Stock may increase*   This can be due to:
  (i) Holding larger quantities of material.
  (ii) Allowing unfinished goods in the form of work-in-progress stock to build up.
  (iii) Holding larger quantities of finished goods.

This increase may be due to lax management control, or the result of necessity, due to greater production being needed to meet increased sales orders. In both cases the result on the cash position will be the same.

(b) *Debtors may increase*   This can be due to:
  (i) Lax control of credit, allowing customers a longer period in which to pay their accounts; or
  (ii) A greater volume of debtors due to higher sales.

In both cases cash resources will be strained.

(c) *Additional investment in fixed assets* This is the most dangerous situation of all. Where cash is tied up in stocks or debtors it will complete the cash flow cycle, and return again as cash in a matter of a few months. Once a fixed asset investment is made, however, the cash will be virtually lost for good. It will only return, in a much reduced form, when the asset is sold, much later on, and at a fraction of the original value.

Cash may also find its way out of the organisation, especially if it is internally generated cash or profit before charging depreciation. Cash may be applied in the following ways.

(a) In payment of dividends to shareholders.
(b) As drawings taken out of a business by its owners if they are sole traders or partners.
(c) In payment of taxation. In the case of a company it will be as corporation tax, and in the case of all other businesses as income tax.
(d) In the repayment of loans.
(e) Being used to reduce the period of credit taken from creditors. This will result in replacing the finance formerly supplied by creditors with the cash resources of the business itself.

Preparation of a Cash Flow Statement

The first task in the preparation of a cash flow (flow of funds) statement is to list the balance sheets at the beginning and the end of the year, and calculate the movement against every heading. Ensure that this movement totals the same amount on both sides of the balance sheet. Take the example of the following balance sheets of Plastic Boxes Limited at 31st December 19-9 and 19-0, with the movement calculated.

	19-9 £	19-0 £	Movement £
Ordinary shares	35 000	42 000	7 000
Profit and Loss Account	15 000	24 000	9 000
Proposed ordinary dividends	7 000	10 000	3 000

	£	£	£
Corporation Tax	12 000	18 000	6 000
Bank overdraft	4 000	—	(4 000)
Creditors	14 000	12 000	(2 000)
	£87 000	£106 000	£19 000
Plant and machinery	45 000	59 000	14 000
Stocks	18 000	10 000	(8 000)
Debtors	24 000	30 000	6 000
Bank balance	—	7 000	7 000
	£87 000	£106 000	£19 000

During the year £9 000 was charged for depreciation on plant and machinery.

The next stage is to understand the full significance of each movement.

Ordinary Shares £7 000 This indicates an increase in issued share capital during the year, with a consequent £7 000 inflow of cash into the business. If there had been a bonus, or scrip, issue, in which reserves were capitalised by the issue of shares, there would have been no inflow of cash. The reserves of the company would, however, have shown a decrease of £7 000.

Profit and Loss Account £9 000 This is the profit retained in the business, after providing for corporation tax and proposed dividends.

Proposed Ordinary Dividends £3 000 The movement of £3 000 masks two separate transactions:

(i) A payment of £7 000 as dividend to the shareholders during this year, which had been included as a provision in the last year's accounts.

(ii) A proposal to pay a dividend of £10 000 during next year, out of this year's profits. A provision for this amount has been included in this year's accounts.

Corporation Tax £6 000 As with proposed ordinary dividends, this movement masks two transactions. There was a provision included in last year's accounts of £12 000, which has been paid during the current year. This year's accounts have a provision of £18 000 included against this year's profits, which will be paid to the Inland Revenue during next year.

In the case of proposed dividends and corporation tax, the provision in the 19-9 accounts will be treated as an application, and that in the 19-0 accounts as a source of cash.

Bank Overdraft £4 000   The overdraft at the beginning of the year has been eliminated and replaced by cash from other sources.

Creditors £2 000   At the end of the year the creditors are financing the business to the extent of £2 000 less than they were at the beginning of the year.

Plant and Machinery £14 000   The investment, after depreciation of £9 000, has increased by £14 000 during the year. This indicates an investment during the year of £23 000 — the increase in the written down value of £14 000 in addition to the depreciation charge of £9 000.

Stock £8 000   The company's resources invested in stock have declined by £8 000 during the year, thus releasing an equivalent amount of cash for investment elsewhere in the business.

Debtors £6 000   The investment of resources in financing debtors has increased by £6 000 during the year, thereby tying up that amount of additional cash resources.

Bank Balance £7 000   This balance at bank has emerged during the year. The figure must be considered in conjunction with the overdraft which stood at £4 000 at the beginning of the year. There has been an improvement of £7 000 plus £4 000 or £11 000 in the cash resources of the company during the year.

Cash Flow or Flow of Funds Statement

The object of this statement is to show:

(*a*)   The sources of cash in the business during the year.
(*b*)   The application of that cash within and without the business.

(c) At the end of the statement the movement during the year of the cash and bank balances.

(a) Sources

The sources of cash may be divided into the following categories:

(i) Internally generated cash, which comprises the retained profit, proposed dividends, the taxation provision, and the depreciation charge.
(ii) Cash introduced from outside sources, in the form of new capital, loans, or further credit granted by suppliers.
(iii) The relocation of cash within the business, coming from a rundown of stock, debtors or fixed assets.

(b) Applications

The cash in the business may be applied in two ways:

(i) By moving outside the business through the payment of dividends or taxation, repayment of loans, or by paying creditors earlier than in the past.
(ii) Through relocation within the business itself, by increasing the investment in fixed assets, stock or debtors.

(c) Cash and Bank Movement

The resultant figure will represent the net inflow or outflow of cash through the bank account.
The statement is presented in the following manner.

Plastic Boxes Ltd
Flow of Funds Statement for the year to 31st December 19-0

Sources:		£	£
Own generation:	Profit & Loss		
	retention	9 000	
	Proposed dividends	10 000	
	Corporation Tax	18 000	
	Depreciation	9 000	
		46 000	
Outside Sources:	Share Issue	7 000	

		£	£
Relocation:	Stock reduction	8 000	
			61 000
Applications:			
Outside:	Dividends paid	7 000	
	Corporation Tax paid	12 000	
	Reduction in creditors	2 000	
Relocation:	Plant and machinery	23 000	
	Debtors increase	6 000	
			50 000
Increase in cash at bank			11 000

Working Capital Movement

This is another way of presenting cash flow information, and in some ways has a greater relevance than the cash flow, or flow of funds statement. To invest in fixed assets is a positive action which a board of directors will only undertake after much consideration. Working capital, on the other hand, is in a constant state of flux. Stock and debtors will be moving every working day, as stock is increased by purchases or production, and then decreased through sales. At the same time debtors will be rising as sales on credit are made, and falling as customers pay their debts. It is very easy for amounts tied up in stocks and debtors to escalate. The investment in working capital must be sufficient to support the level of turnover that is being achieved — but it must not be allowed to become excessive. Close attention must be paid to this aspect, and a working capital movement statement helps to control it.

The method is identical to that of the previous statement except that the final balance is not bank movement, but working capital movement. The sources and applications will be confined to those items that are not to be found in working capital. These items cover internally generated cash, outside sources of cash, and relocation of cash from fixed assets or investments only. The applications will be outside the business, or relocation into fixed assets only. The balance remaining will represent the working capital movement, which is then analysed between stock, debtors, bank and creditors. The object here is to show how the resources of the business have been tied up in financing working capital, which happens when current assets increase, and conversely to show when they have been released, to be invested elsewhere in the business, or to be withdrawn from the organisation altogether.

The statement will appear as follows, using the information for Plastic Boxes Ltd given earlier.

Plastic Boxes Ltd
Statement of working capital movement
for the year to 31st December 19-0

		£	£
Sources:			
Own generation:	Profit & Loss retention	9 000	
	Proposed dividends	10 000	
	Corporation Tax	18 000	
	Depreciation	9 000	
		46 000	
Outside Sources:	Share Issue	7 000	
			53 000
Applications:			
Outside:	Dividends paid	7 000	
	Corporation Tax paid	12 000	
		19 000	
Relocation:	Plant and machinery	23 000	
			42 000
Increase in working capital			£11 000

Analysis of increase in working capital

Increases:	Debtors increase	6 000
	Creditors reduction	2 000
	Bank increase	11 000
		19 000
Decreases:	Stock reduction	8 000
Net increase in working capital		£11 000

The fact that a reduction in creditors is treated as an increase in working capital may cause some confusion. Creditors have, in effect, withdrawn finance from the business which must now be made good from the company's own internal resources.

When flow of funds statements are being prepared, it is necessary to organise them on the basis of where cash has come from (sources) and where it has gone to (applications). This creates a far better impression than remembering a format and merely filling in figures to fit it. In the above example, if there had been a capital reduction, instead of an increase in the number of shares in issue, it should have been dealt with as an application of cash, rather than a negative source.

Assignments

13.1. Do you consider that a cash flow statement is necessary for the proper understanding of the financial position of a business?

13.2. The following is a summary of the balance sheets of Smith Tools Ltd for the two years to 30th April 19-0. Depreciation charged for the year to 30th April 19-0 was £6 000.

	19-0 £	19-9 £
Ordinary shares	30 000	25 000
Profit & Loss Account	24 000	17 000
Proposed ordinary dividend	8 000	4 000
Long-term loan @ 12%	—	15 000
Corporation Tax	12 000	9 000
Bank overdraft	8 000	—
Creditors	15 000	11 000
	£97 000	£81 000
Plant and machinery	62 000	45 000
Stocks	14 000	11 000
Debtors	21 000	18 000
Bank balance	—	7 000
	£97 000	£81 000

PREPARE: (1) A cash flow(flow of funds) statement
(2) A working capital movement statement
for the year to 30th April 19-0.

13.3. How does a business acquire cash, and how can it apply that cash in the day to day running of its affairs?

13.4. You have been running a small manufacturing company for the past ten years, operating from old and decrepit premises in a demolition area. The area is due for redevelopment, and you have decided to buy a new factory ten miles from your old premises, with the help of a bank overdraft. What cash flow problems can you expect, and how would you attempt to overcome them?

13.5. You are the managing director of Optimistic Optics Ltd. Nine months ago your bank manager granted you overdraft facilities of £80 000 in order to purchase empty factory premises next to your existing ones. You persuaded him that the project was viable.

Recently you submitted your accounts for the year to 30th September 19-2 to the bank manager. He has presented flow of funds statements, and has written to you suggesting an immediate interview.

Your balance sheets for the past two years are:

	19-2 £	19-1 £
Ordinary Shares	50 000	50 000
Profit & Loss account	65 000	80 000
Proposed ordinary dividends	—	13 000
Corporation Tax	—	17 000
Bank overdraft	81 000	—
Creditors	60 000	32 000
	£256 000	£192 000
Plant and Machinery at cost	70 000	30 000
Less Depreciation	(28 000)	(19 000)
Premises at cost	120 000	50 000
Stocks	30 000	25 000
Debtors	64 000	73 000

	£	£
Bank balance	—	33 000
	£256 000	£192 000

Your sales over the past two years have been static.

REQUIRED:

(1) Prepare a cash flow statement to illustrate the decline in your bank balance.
(2) Prepare a working capital movement statement to show the movement in working capital during the year.
(3) What has caused your problems?
(4) Why do you think the bank manager wishes to see you?
(5) What solutions to the problem can you suggest?

14. Profitability

Profitability is the essence of business. Without it a progressive decline will set in that will, in time, lead to the extinction of the organisation. Stop for a moment to consider the obligations of business.

(a) The persons who have supplied the capital with which the business has been established are entitled to a return on that money. The return can only be provided by making an adequate profit.

(b) The employees of a business who are devoting their lives and skills in return for an income, are entitled to look forward — if they should so desire it — to a continuity of income and employment. Moreover, the income should be reasonable in view of the skills that are being shown by the employees. This security can only be realised if adequate profitability is being achieved.

(c) The future income of shareholders and employees can only be assured if the business keeps abreast of modern developments, by investing in new plant and processes. This can only take place if there is sufficient profit being made to finance that investment.

(d) There is, finally, the obligation of the business to society in general. A business will be expected to pay a fairly large share of local and central government expenditure. This it will do in the form of rates and taxes. Rates will be borne more easily by a profitable business, and taxation will only be payable by a profitable business. The burden of being unpaid tax collector for Value Added Tax and Pay As You Earn which falls on all businesses can be absorbed more easily by the profitable, than by the unprofitable business.

In what does the profitability of a business lie? Basically, it can only be achieved if there is a secure turnover. This must, however, be allied to a selling price that is sufficiently high to enable a profit to be made. The best method of understanding this is to use the principles of marginal costing. This maintains that there are two types of cost.

(*a*) *Variable costs*, which will only be incurred when production takes place. These costs include direct labour, direct materials, power used to drive machinery, consumable items and a host of others.

(*b*) *Fixed costs*, which will be incurred regardless of the level of turnover. These cover such charges as depreciation of machinery, rent and rates, lighting and heating and salaries.

You will recall from an earlier chapter that in marginal costing fixed overheads are not allocated, but are kept in bulk. Variable costs alone are allocated to product, and the difference between the selling price of the product and the variable or marginal cost, is called a contribution, which in total is available to meet the unallocated fixed overheads.

Profitability can now be seen to arise from the interaction of three forces.

(*a*) Achieving as high a contribution as possible from each unit of production that is sold. This implies manufacturing as cheaply as possible, consistent with maintaining quality, and striving for as high a selling price as the market will stand.

(*b*) Keeping all fixed overhead charges to the lowest possible level.

(*c*) Selling as many units of production as possible.

To keep these three elements in balance is no easy task. Variable costs can be affected by material price and wage rate increases; poor production methods causing excessive scrap; and low morale amongst the work force. The selling price is ultimately governed by what the market will stand. If the market price for an item is £5, the selling price must be brought into line, and it will only be possible to sell at a price fractionally higher if quality and delivery are better than that of competitors. The number of units sold will depend on quality, delivery and price. If it is desired to increase the share of the market, it can only be done at the expense of competitors. Quality and delivery will obviously help to woo customers from existing sources of supply that are giving poor service and poor quality. If the market share thus acquired is not sufficient, the only other way is to cut price. Once that happens, the unit contribution drops. It will drop not by the percentage cut in selling price, but by the percentage that the monetary drop in selling price bears to the value of the unit contribution. Take as an example a product that is being sold for £1 with a marginal cost of 60p. It is then decided to drop the selling price by 5% to 95p. The margin will then drop to 35p from 40p, a fall of 12½%. It will now be necessary to sell over 14¼% more units to achieve the same contribution as before. If 100 000 units were being sold before the price decrease, the overall contribution would have been 100 000 × 40p = £40 000. In order to achieve a similar contribution at the new price, the number of units to be sold will have to be $\frac{£40\,000}{0.35}$ = 114 286 units, an increase of 14.29%.

Prices should, therefore, only be cut as a last resort, and then only when management is confident that there will be a sufficient increase in turnover to give an increased contribution.

Finally, there is the position of fixed overheads. If they increase in total, as a result of salary increases, higher rents and rates, lighting and heating, or any other of the many elements making up the overall charge, more contribution will be needed to cover them. Greater contribution can come in four ways.

(a) Raising the selling price.
(b) Lowering the marginal cost.
(c) Selling more items.
(d) Reducing some of the other elements in fixed overheads, as a result of a cost reduction exercise.

The final result may be a combination of all four. There is no easy, straightforward answer to profitability. It is a matter of continual vigilance at all times, checking the warning signs as they appear, and taking appropriate correcting action straight away.

Stock Evaluation

Methods of stock evaluation have already been studied. It is now necessary to appreciate the effect that stock evaluation can have on the profitability of a business.

Stock represents goods that have been purchased during an accounting period, but have not been sold when that period ends. They will therefore, be available for use or sale during the next accounting period. The closing stock of one period thus becomes the opening stock of the next. Stock, in this sense, becomes a vehicle for carrying forward cost from one accounting period into the next. Strictly, the transfer should be the cost of the stock, but that is a difficult value to establish.

The easiest type of stock to evaluate is that of a factoring organisation which buys completed units, and then sells them to its customers. At first glance there is no problem — merely evaluate at the price charged on the invoice. This is a simple task if stores records have been maintained based upon LIFO, FIFO or AvCo, but more difficult if no records have been maintained, and it is not known when the stock was purchased.

Where a business is manufacturing, the problems become immense, and several methods of stock evaluation have been used.

(a) Evaluate at material cost only.
(b) Evaluate at prime cost i.e. direct material, direct labour and direct expenses.
(c) Evaluate at works cost, the justification being that without a factory, and the costs of running it, production could not take place.
(d) Evaluate at full cost, excluding only those items of general overheads that are incurred after production is complete, such as selling and delivery expenses. Sometimes a case is even made out for including selling expenses were production is only commenced when the order has already been received.

In the case of long-term contracts in which final completion stretches over several years, problems of stock evaluation are even greater. It is important that excessive profit is not taken during any interim accounting period. Profit is released on a very conservative basis until the completion of the contract. It frequently happens that costs build up rapidly during the final months of a contract, when overtime working can be needed to meet the completion deadline. This can result in a final loss if too much profit has been released in earlier periods.

136 Accounting for Management

In recent years the major accountancy bodies have issued statements of standard accounting practice, and the guidance given for stock evaluation is to include all expenditure that has been incurred in bringing the product to its present stage of completion. This includes all related production overheads, even though some of them may be of a fixed nature. This should give an element of consistency to the problem of valuing stock. There has, however, been some opposition to this new method, as any change in the method of stock evaluation has an immediate effect upon the profits that a business declares. It is not a method of creating more — or less — profit in the long term. No matter how many times a business varies its method of valuing stock during its lifetime, it will not in the slightest affect the overall profit made. It is, however a method of adjusting profit between accounting periods. For this reason it is important that there be stability in the methods used. Where changes are made they should be fully publicised in the accounts.

To illustrate this point, take the example of Packing Cases Ltd, manufacturers of a standard-sized wooden pallet. The company commenced trading on 1st January 19-8, and closed down on 31st December 19-0. Its costs for each period were:

		19-8	19-9	19-0
Unit costs:	Materials	£5	£6	£7
	Labour	£2	£3	£4
Overheads:	Works	£15 000	£20 000	£25 000
	General	£25 000	£40 000	£50 000
Pallets produced		20 000	30 000	25 000
Pallets sold		15 000	32 000	28 000
Unit selling price		£10	£12	£14

Calculate the profits declared each year if stock is valued at
  (a) Prime cost.
  (b) Factory cost.

Stock records are kept on a FIFO basis.

  (i) The first task is to calculate the stock units.

Stock in units

	19-8	19-9	19-0
Opening stock	—	5 000	3 000
Production	20 000	30 000	25 000
	20 000	35 000	28 000
Sales	15 000	32 000	28 000
Closing Stock	5 000	3 000	—

These stock figures will be basic to both calculations.

(ii) Next calculate the results of valuing the stock on the basis of prime cost.

	19-8 £	19-9 £	19-0 £
Prime cost per unit —			
Materials	5	6	7
Labour	2	3	4
	7	9	11
Cost of production			
20 000 × £7	140 000	—	—
30 000 × £9	—	270 000	—
25 000 × £11	—	—	275 000
Value of stock			
5 000 × £7	35 000	—	—
3 000 × £9	—	27 000	—
Sales			
15 000 × £10	150 000	—	—
32 000 × £12	—	384 000	—
28 000 × £14	—	—	392 000

From the above information, the operating statement for each year can be prepared.

138 Accounting for Management

	19-8 £	£	19-9 £	£	19-0 £	£
Sales		150 000		384 000		392 000
Less Cost of Sales:						
Opening stock	—		35 000		27 000	
Add Production:						
Prime cost	140 000		270 000		275 000	
Works o'heads	15 000		20 000		25 000	
	155 000		325 000		327 000	
Less Closing stock	35 000		27 000		—	
		120 000		298 000		327 000
Gross profit		30 000		86 000		65 000
Less General overheads		25 000		40 000		50 000
Net profit		£5 000		£46 000		£15 000

(iii) To calculate the results of valuing stock with factory overheads included, the stock must be recomputed. The unit cost of works overheads will be found by dividing the yearly figure of works overhead by the relevant production.

$$19\text{-}8 \quad \frac{£15\ 000}{20\ 000} = 75\text{p per unit.}$$

$$19\text{-}9 \quad \frac{£20\ 000}{30\ 000} = 67\text{p per unit.}$$

$$19\text{-}0 \quad \frac{£25\ 000}{25\ 000} = £1.00 \text{ per unit.}$$

This will give unit costs for stock evaluation purposes of:

19-8 £7.00 plus £0.75 = £7.75
19-9 £9.00 plus £0.67 = £9.67

The value of stock will now be:

19-8 5 000 × £7.75 = £38 750
19-9 3 000 × £9.67 = £29 010

The operating statements will appear as below.

	19-8		19-9		19-0	
	£	£	£	£	£	£
Sales		150 000		384 000		392 000
Less Cost of sales:						
Opening stock	—		38 750		29 010	
Add Prime cost	140 000		270 000		275 000	
Works o'head	15 000		20 000		25 000	
	155 000		328 750		329 010	
Less Closing stock	38 750		29 010		—	
		116 250		299 740		329 010
Gross profit		33 750		84 260		62 990
Less General overheads		25 000		40 000		50 000
Net profit		£8 750		£44 260		£12 990

The total profits declared are the same in both cases:

	Prime cost method £	Works cost method £
19-8	5 000	8 750
19-9	46 000	44 260
19-0	15 000	12 990
	£66 000	£66 000

This proves that the effect of stock valuation on different bases is cosmetic only, and does not affect the amount of profit actually made in the long term.

Assignments

14.1. The firm of which you are the management accountant has suffered a fall in sales. With it has come a large fall in profits. The managing director is puzzled, and has asked you to report to him as follows.

(a) What could have caused the large fall in profits relative to the fall in sales?

(b) What can be done to rectify the position?

Draft your report.

14.2. How can a business achieve profitability? Illustrate your answer with examples.

14.3. Irripumps Ltd manufactures an irrigation pump which sells for £100, with a marginal cost of £70. Monthly fixed overheads are £32 000. The pump is sold extensively in the Middle East, and monthly sales are 1 000 units.

The sales director has just returned from a visit to the Middle East with the news that during a recent six week strike, which completely disrupted Irripumps' deliveries, a Japanese manufacturer has produced a similar pump, slightly less reliable, which sells for £96. The sales director has proposed dropping the selling price of the pump by 5%, which will give an estimated increase in sales of 10% 'and that must re-establish our profitability, and make us competitive'. The managing director has asked you for your opinion. How would you reply?

14.4. You are the company secretary of Hardslog Ltd, a subsidiary company of a large group. The managing director has recently returned from a meeting with the chairman of the group, who is looking for increasing profits from Hardslog over the next five years. Your accounts and budgets indicate that it is unlikely that this profit level will be reached.

The managing director has called a board meeting to discuss methods of increasing the profitability of the company. The works director suggests that, as stock is at present valued at prime cost only, profit can be increased each year by including all overheads in the valuation. The managing director, seeing a way out of his problems, asks you why you have not thought of 'such a brilliant idea'. How would you reply?

14.5. Pitt Products Limited commenced business on 1st June 19-7, and prepared accounts for the years to 31st May 19-7, 19-8 and 19-9. You are given the following information.

(a) Stock records are maintained on a FIFO basis.

		19-7	19-8	19-9
(b)	Unit costs are: Material	£3	£4	£5
	Labour	£2	£3	£4
(c)	Production (in units)	30 000	39 000	45 000

(d)	Sales (in units)	24 000	42 000	46 000
(e)	Works overhead	£40 000	£52 000	£60 000
(f)	General overheads	£60 000	£70 000	£80 000
(g)	Selling price	£10	£11	£12

REQUIRED:
Prepare operating statements for each of the three years to show the effect on profit of valuing stock on the following bases:

(a) Prime cost.
(b) Works cost, incorporating 75% of works overheads only.

15. Ratio Analysis

The prime task of an accountant is to present his information in such a way that it can be understood by people who are not well versed in figures. Masses of figures will merely confuse, so a method has to be used that will present the essential facts of the situation in as simple a manner as possible. Ratio analysis is the method used. The significance of the relationship of figures to each other is expressed as a simple ratio. In isolation the figures mean little. Once a series of figures has been built up over a period of months or years, trends become apparent. This can be of great help to general management in its attempt to control a business. A further advantage comes from inter-firm comparison. The results of other businesses, when presented in the form of ratios, enable comparison to be made with similar ratios in one's own business. The ratios must be constructed in the same way in each business. They give a valid basis of comparison, without revealing too much of the detail of the inner workings of the business.

Different ratios appeal to different people. Management, having the task of running a business efficiently, will be interested in all ratios. A supplier of goods on credit will be particularly interested in liquidity ratios, which indicate the ability of the business to pay its bills. Existing and future shareholders will be interested in investment ratios, which indicate the level of return that can be expected on an investment in the business. Major customers, intent on having a continuing source of supply, will be interested in the financial stability, as revealed by the capital structure, liquidity and profitability ratios. Debenture and loan stock holders will be interested in the ability of a business to pay interest, and ultimately to repay the capital. A banker, giving only short-term loans, will be interested mainly in the liquidity of the business, and its ability to repay those loans.

The overall advantage of ratios is that they enable valid comparisons to be made between businesses of varying size, and in different industries. It is very difficult to compare the accounts of a shop having one branch with a multi-branch giant like Marks & Spencer. The former could have assets of less than a hundred thousand pounds, while the assets of the latter could be many hundreds of millions of pounds. The smaller firm would look puny compared to the giant, yet its profitability, use of assets and liquidity could all be much stronger. Ratio analysis will help to reveal this.

It must not be thought, however, that all the problems of a business can be solved by ratio analysis. It will merely give a general indication of a trend, at the same time spotlighting any divergence from normality. This knowledge, however, should enable management to correct whatever may be going wrong in the business.

Ratios can be illustrated from the following abridged accounts of Wiseman Ltd for the year to 31st December 19-0.

Trading & Profit & Loss Account
for the year to 31st December 19-0

	£	£
Sales		980 000
Less Cost of sales: Opening stock	90 000	
Add Purchases	651 000	
	741 000	
Less Closing stock	100 000	641 000
		339 000
Less General administration		220 000
Net operating profit		119 000
Less Debenture interest	12 000	
Loan interest	5 000	17 000
		102 000
Add Copyright income		500
Profit before taxation		102 500

144 *Accounting for Management*

	£	£
Corporation Tax		50 000
Net profit after taxation		52 500
Less Dividends — Preference Shares	2 500	
— Ordinary Shares	20 000	22 500
Profit retained for the year		30 000
Add Balance from previous years		20 000
Balance carried to Balance Sheet		£50 000

(See Balance Sheet opposite.)

Ratios may be classified according to the aspect of the business that is being highlighted.

A. Profitability Ratios

These attempt to illustrate the profitability — or otherwise — of the business. Profitability is the most commonly accepted method of assessing the efficiency of the management of a business. The following ratios are used.

(1) *Rate of Gross Profit*

This ratio is expressed as a percentage, and is calculated from the formula:

$$\frac{\text{Gross profit}}{\text{Sales}} \times 100$$

Substituting the figures from the accounts of Wiseman Ltd, we get:

$$\frac{£339\ 000}{£980\ 000} \times 100 = 34.6\%$$

The higher that this percentage is, the better the performance of the business.

(2) *Rate of Net Profit*

Once more this is expressed as a percentage from the formula:

$$\frac{\text{Net profit}}{\text{Sales}} \times 100$$

Ratio Analysis

Balance Sheet at 31st December 19-0

Share capital	Authorised £	Issued £				
200 000 £1 Ordinary Shares	200 000	200 000				
50 000 £1 5% Preference Shares	50 000	50 000				
	250 000	250 000				
Reserves:						
Profit & Loss Account		50 000				
		300 000				
Long-term liabilities:						
8% Debentures	150 000					
10% Loan Stock	50 000	200 000				
Current liabilities:						
Trade creditors	70 000					
Taxation	40 000					
Dividends	20 000	130 000				
		£630 000				

	Cost £	Dep'n. £	£
Fixed Assets			
Buildings	400 000	100 000	300 000
Plant etc.	120 000	40 000	80 000
	520 000	140 000	380 000
Current assets:			
Stock		100 000	
Debtors		145 000	
Cash at bank		5 000	250 000
			£630 000

Market price of the ordinary shares, £1.40 per share.

146 *Accounting for Management*

Again substituting the Wiseman figures we get

$$\frac{£102\ 500}{£980\ 000} \times 100 = 10.5\%$$

A low return on sales does not necessarily indicate inefficiency, as there may be a very rapid turnover of stock with a small profit margin, as in food supermarkets. It is, therefore, necessary to look at another aspect of profitability.

(3) *Return on Capital Employed*

The formula for this ratio is:

$$\frac{\text{Net profit before loan interest}}{\text{Capital employed}} \times 100$$

The capital employed includes not only the shareholders' funds, but also long-term liabilities. The net profit must be increased by the amount of interest paid to the holders of loan or debenture stock. This gives the profit that has arisen from the use of all the capital invested in the business.

In the Wiseman example the profit figure is £102 500 + £17 000 = £119 500. Total capital employed is £300 000 + £200 000 = £500 000.

This gives a ratio of $\quad \dfrac{£119\ 500}{£500\ 000} \times 100 = 23.9\%$

This indicates the efficiency with which the business is being managed. Management must always try to earn the greatest possible return on the capital invested in the business. If profit increases, yet capital employed increases by an even greater percentage, the fact will be revealed by a fall in this ratio.

(4) *Net Profit after Tax/Owners' Equity*

Taxation is a charge that can vary from year to year depending — amongst other things — on the investment policy of the firm. If much new plant has been purchased, with correspondingly high capital allowances, the taxation charge will be very small or non-existent. If however, there has been little capital investment, the taxation charge will be much higher. The figure of net profit after taxation is, therefore, not a true reflection of the performance of the management team. It is, however, important in assessing the net return on shareholders' funds, as it is out of this taxed profit that dividends are paid.

The equity (ordinary) shareholders own all the accumulated reserves as well as the issued ordinary share capital. The ratio will be

$$\frac{\text{Net profit after tax less preference dividends}}{\text{Ordinary shares + Reserves}} \times 100$$

In the case of Wiseman, this will be

$$\frac{£50\,000}{£250\,000} \times 100 = 20\%$$

B. Liquidity Ratios

The next area to consider is that of liquidity, or the ability of a business to pay its way. These ratios are concerned with the working capital, or the relationship between current assets and current liabilities. There are two main liquidity ratios.

(1) Current Ratio

This is the relationship between current assets and current liabilities, and is calculated by dividing current liabilities into current assets. The ratio shows the number of times that current liabilities are covered by current assets. In the Wiseman example, the ratio is:

$$\frac{£250\,000}{£130\,000} = 1.92 \text{ times.}$$

This indicates that there is over 90% surplus cover for the current liabilities, and the business appears to be adequately solvent. The underlying figures may yet give cause for concern. A much more stringent test must, therefore, be applied.

(2) Acid Test Ratio

This is a ratio based upon current liabilities and current assets exclusive of stock, as stock can only be converted into cash after sale, and a further period will elapse before payment is received from the resulting debtors. The ratio is concerned only with 'quick' assets — those that are already in the form of cash, or can easily and quickly be converted into it. The ratio results from the following formula:

In the Wiseman example, the ratio is $\dfrac{\text{Quick assets}}{\text{Current liabilities}}$

$\dfrac{£150\,000}{£130\,000} = 1.15$ times.

This is vastly different from the current ratio, as Wiseman's stock formed 40% of the current assets.

The significance of the ratio is to reveal the extent of the readily available cover, if all the current liabilities were to press for immediate payment. Although bank overdrafts are normally negotiated for a twelve month period, immediate repayment is demanded when it is suspected that a bank's customer is becoming financially embarassed. The overdraft then becomes a very current liability. For a healthy position a business should have an acid test ratio in the region of 1. Much will depend on the type of business, and some could cope with a smaller ratio than others. If the ratio exceeds 1 by too large a margin, it could be a sign of inefficiency, with too much being tied up in quick current assets.

C. Asset Usage Ratios

Management and shareholders are interested in the efficiency with which assets are employed in the business. The return made on those assets must be sufficient to compensate for the risks involved in running a business.

(1) *Collection Period for Debtors*

This is a most important ratio. It is very easy for debtors to expand out of hand. Each day sales are being made, and customers are paying their debts. Unless there is an effective credit control policy, debtors will take extended credit, and the finance required to support them will increase alarmingly. A simple plotting of this ratio will prove a simple and efficient indicator of the effectiveness of credit control.

The ratio is expressed as the number of days average sales that is outstanding, based upon a 365 day year. The annual sales are divided by 365 to give an average day's sales. This figure is then divided into the debtors to form the ratio. In the example, annual sales are £980 000, and debtors £145 000. Average daily sales are

$$\dfrac{£980\,000}{365} = £2\,685$$

Debtors outstanding in days will be:

$$\frac{£145\ 000}{£\ 2\ 685} = 54 \text{ days}.$$

In the absence of a discount incentive, debtors of approximately 60 days can be expected even in the most efficient of companies.

(2) Stock Turnover Ratio

This again is a useful ratio as it helps to control a sector of a business that can also very easily get out of hand. Whenever stock is built up it diverts cash from the bank account to pay for it. This can lead to a shortage of liquid resources. Stock is less easy than debtors to turn into cash, and is subject to deterioration if kept for long periods.

The ratio indicates the number of times that the stock is used, or turned over, during a year. The year end stockholding is no true indication of average stockholding during the year. If the stock of each month is known, and averaged, a good idea of average stockholding will be possible. Failing that, the next best thing is to average opening and closing stocks for the year, by adding them together, and dividing by two. This average stock is then divided into the cost of sales for the year, to reveal the number of times that average stock has been turned over during the year. If only the annual sales figure is available, rather than the cost of sales, it must be used. The ratio will then be understated, because of the inclusion of a profit element in sales.

In the Wiseman example, opening stock is £90 000, closing stock £100 000 and the cost of sales for the year £641 000. The average

stock is £90 000 + £100 000 = $\frac{£190\ 000}{2}$ = £95 000.

The ratio is $\frac{£641\ 000}{£\ 95\ 000}$ = 6.7 times.

It is impossible to give a ratio that will indicate a satisfactory situation in all cases. Much will depend on the type of business. A department store will turn its stock over much more slowly than a foundry which is producing castings only when it receives an order from a customer. Again, the length of time taken to produce the product will affect the amount of stock that must be carried, as will the length of time taken to replace raw material stock.

(3) Sales/Fixed Assets

This ratio indicates that efficiency with which fixed assets are being used to generate sales. It is calculated by dividing fixed assets into the sales, and is expressed as the number of times that sales cover fixed assets. In the example the ratio is:

$$\frac{£980\ 000}{£380\ 000} = 2.6 \text{ times.}$$

A low ratio indicates that management may be inefficient in its utilisation of fixed assets. The size of the ratio depends largely on the type of business. A large capital investment results in a relatively low ratio. On the other hand a labour intensive industry, employing much hand labour, should result in a high ratio.

D. Capital Structure Ratios

These ratios indicate the effect of gearing on the dividend policy of a company, and also the risk that lenders face when advancing loans. Gearing is a method of financing a business partly by ordinary shares, and partly by fixed interest shares or loan stock. A company that is high-geared has a high proportion of its capital in fixed-interest securities. In years of good profit, where the rate of earnings exceeds the fixed interest or dividend payable, the ordinary shareholders will benefit from the surplus profit. Where the earnings are little more than or fall below the high fixed interest payable, the ordinary shareholders must subsidise the fixed interest stockholders, and take a lower rate of dividend, or by-pass it altogether.

(1) Cover for Fixed Charges

This ratio indicates the cover that exists for fixed charges. Loan and debenture stock interest is a normal charge against profits, and appears as a charge in the profit and loss account. The figure of profit before tax must be inflated by the interest charges to calculate the amount available to pay those fixed charges. The ratio is expressed as the number of times cover that exists for the fixed charges. Wiseman's profit is £102 500, and with interest charges of £17 000 becomes £119 500. This gives a ratio of

$$\frac{£119\ 500}{£\ 17\ 000} = 7.0 \text{ times.}$$

This is adequate cover for the loan stock interest, even allowing for a fall in profits.

(2) Net Worth/Total Assets

Net worth is the total value invested in a business by the shareholders. It is calculated by adding together all the issued share capital — both ordinary and preference — and the total reserves. Total assets comprise fixed and current assets. The ratio will show the percentage of total assets financed by the shareholders. In the illustration the shareholders' investment totals £300 000, out of total assets of £630 000. The ratio is:

$$\frac{£300\ 000}{£630\ 000} \times 100 = 47.6\%$$

Such a low percentage could form a bar to future borrowings, until the shareholders have a larger stake in the business. A business always represents a risk. In the above case the shareholders are taking the risk to a large extent with the capital of non-shareholders. Few lenders are happy until the shareholders have financed the majority of the assets of a business.

(3) Net Worth/Fixed Assets

This ratio assesses the extent to which shareholders' funds are used to finance the fixed assets of the business. Like the previous ratio, it is expressed as a percentage. Wiseman's net worth has already been calculated as £300 000, and the investment in fixed assets is £380 000. The ratio is

$$\frac{£300\ 000}{£380\ 000} \times 100 = 78.9\%$$

Potential lenders to a business will be unhappy with a situation where shareholders' funds are insufficient to finance even the fixed assets. Further borrowings will depend upon an increase in the shareholders' stake in the business.

E. Investment Ratios

These ratios are important for existing and potential investors in a company, and also for top management, responsible for the overall

152 Accounting for Management

Stock Exchange rating of the shares. When an investor buys shares in a company, it is usually done to obtain an income in the form of dividends. Shares are issued at varying nominal values. The company will have decided to issue shares to a certain value, and this value can then be broken down into shares of £1, 50p, 25p, 20p, 10p, or even 5p, according to company policy. If it is a public company which has applied to the Stock Exchange for a quotation, the shares will find a ready market. The investor can then find a purchaser should he desire to sell his shares. When shares change hands, however, they rarely do so at their nominal value. If the business has been successful, the price will be in excess of the nominal — or par — value. If the recent results of the company have been poor, the price may well be below par. When dividends are declared, the percentage rate is based on the nominal value of the shares. The purchase price, however, will probably differ from par. The return on the investment will then differ from the rate of dividend declared. It is these apparent anomalies that investment ratios attempt to clarify.

(1) Earnings per Ordinary Share

This indicates the profitability of the company, and gives the percentage return on the ordinary shares that is available for payment of dividends and/or retention in the company. Profit is taken after tax, and after paying preference dividends. Wiseman's net profit is £52 500, with preference dividends payable of £2 500. The number of £1 ordinary shares is 200 000. The ratio is:

$$\frac{£52\ 500 - £2\ 500}{200\ 000} = \frac{£50\ 000}{200\ 000}$$

$$= £0.25 \text{ per share, a return of } 25\%$$

(2) Ordinary Share Dividend Cover

The cover for the ordinary dividend is indicated by this ratio. The net profit after tax and preference dividends is divided by the total amount of dividend payable on ordinary shares. In the example the total ordinary dividend is £20 000, and the ratio is

$$\frac{£50\ 000}{£20\ 000} = 2.5 \text{ times.}$$

This suggests a sound position with adequate dividend cover.

(3) Dividend Yield

This ratio converts the rate of dividend declared on the nominal value of shares, into the yield that the investor receives on his investment. It is calculated by dividing the monetary value of the dividend by the market value paid for the share, and multiplying by 100. The figures in the example are:

$$\frac{£1 \times 10\%}{£1.40} \times 100 = \frac{£0.10}{£1.40} \times 100 = 7.1\%$$

If a purchase of shares has already been made, the price of the purchase will be used as the market price. If, however, a purchase is contemplated, the expected market price will be used.

(4) Price/Earnings Ratio

This is a ratio much used in the investment world, and is published daily for each quoted share. It links the earnings per share with the market price, and shows the number of years' purchase of those earnings that the market price represents. In the Wiseman example the earnings per ordinary share have already been calculated (1 above) at 25p. The market price is £1.40, and the price/earnings (P/E) ratio is:

$$\frac{£1.40}{£0.25} = 5.6 \text{ times.}$$

The ratio is a good indicator of the market evaluation of the future prospects of the company. Generally a low P/E ratio suggests lack of confidence, while a high one indicates great confidence. There are weaknesses in P/E ratios. The earnings per share are based upon the last published accounts, whereas the market price of the shares is up to date, and has been adjusted by all subsequent information disclosed about the company's prospects. A very low profit in the last accounts, allied to a modest rise in market price on the expectation of better results in the coming year, can give a high P/E ratio. This might indicate a stronger position than is actually the case.

Assignments

15.1. What ratios will management be interested in, and why?

15.2. You are contemplating an investment in a quoted company.

What ratios will you be interested in? Explain the significance of each.

15.3. A business has the following current assets,

	£
Stock	90 000
Debtors	109 000
Cash in hand	1 000

and current liabilities

Creditors	106 000
Overdraft	25 000

It requires a further increase in overdraft facilities.
(a) From the above information calculate whatever ratios you can for presentation to the bank manager.
(b) Do they reveal a strong liquid position?
(c) What other ratios will the bank manager require before making his decision?

15.4. You have discovered that ZY Ltd had a stockturn ratio of 9 during the year to 30th June 19-5. Its turnover for the year was £240 000, and its gross margin was 33⅓% of cost of sales. The stock at the beginning of the year was £18 000. What was the closing stock?

15.5. The accounts of the Ragbag Trading Company Ltd for the year to 31st December 19-6 were:

Summarised Profit & Loss Account for the year to 31st December 19-6

	£	£
Sales		800 000
Less Cost of sales		608 000
Gross profit		192 000
Less General expenses	100 000	
Loan interest	20 000	120 000
Net profit		72 000

	£	£
Less Taxation		20 000
		52 000
Less Dividends		40 000
Retained profit		12 000
Add Balance from previous year		58 000
Balance carried to Balance Sheet		£70 000

Balance Sheet at 31st December 19-6

	£	£	£
Capital			
Authorised and Issued:			
400 000 Ordinary Shares of £1			400 000
Reserves: Retained profit			70 000
Shareholders' capital			470 000
10% Loan stock			200 000
Capital employed			£670 000
Represented by:			
Fixed Assets: Premises			300 000
Machinery			150 000
Furniture etc.			80 000
Vehicles			40 000
			570 000
Current assets: Stock		70 000	
Debtors		120 000	
		190 000	
Less Current liabilities:			
Creditors	40 000		
Bank overdraft	50 000	90 000	100 000
			£670 000

The stock at the beginning of the year was £82 000.
The £1 ordinary shares are quoted at £1.30 on the Stock Exchange.

REQUIRED:

(1) Calculate ratios to illustrate the following aspects of the company:

(*a*) Profitability
(*b*) Liquidity
(*c*) Asset usage
(*d*) Capital structure
(*e*) Investment potential of the shares.

(2) What is your overall impression of the soundness of the company?

15.6. The debtor ratio of BA Limited at 30th April 19-8 was 78 days. Sales for the year were £1 826 825.

If the debtor ratio had been reduced to 69 days, by how much would cash resources have been improved?

16. Presentation of Information

In many ways the management accountant is the provider of information in an organisation, with the accounts department acting as the information centre. Much time and effort goes into the collection of information, and the form of presentation has a great influence upon the use to which that information is put. There are few things more frustrating than to spend much time collecting information together, only to find that it is never used. Some people have a deep-rooted inability to understand the true significance of figures. Often this is due to the slip-shod manner in which much information is presented. The management accountant can make his — or her — job much more interesting, satisfying and rewarding by concentrating upon the method of presentation, and altering that presentation according to the abilities of the recipient.

The greater the mass of figures presented, the greater can be the confusion. Yet it is possible to convey the significance of figures by an orderly presentation, or even in graphical or diagrammatical form.

Tables

It is important to present figures in a manner that will convey their significance. Much thought must go into this task, as a poorly presented table can be as confusing as a jumble of figures. A decision must be made as to the purpose of the table, and it should be constructed with that in mind.

There are also several basic principles to be followed if the resulting table is to prove satisfactory.

158 *Accounting for Management*

- (*a*) Above all it must be simple. If it aims to cover too wide a field, or present too much detail, its effect will be lost, and confusion may result.
- (*b*) The source of the information should be clearly stated, preferably as a footnote.
- (*c*) There must always be a title to the table, to give an indication of the contents.
- (*d*) Where titles are given to columns and rows, they must be completely free from ambiguity.
- (*e*) It is best to avoid double counting, whereby the same information is presented under more than one heading in the same table.
- (*f*) The units of which the table is constructed (£s, metres, kilos etc.) should be clearly stated.
- (*g*) If the table could be improved by the addition of rates and percentages, they should be included.
- (*h*) Totals and sub-totals should be shown where their inclusion would aid the presentation of the information.

A soundly constructed table will have some distinct advantages over an unorganised listing of data.

- (*a*) It has the very practical advantage that it takes up less room, as many items of a like nature will be grouped together.
- (*b*) A table facilitates comparison between different classes of data.
- (*c*) Figures can be located much more readily than if they are merely listed in a disorganised manner.
- (*d*) Patterns within the figures can be easily discovered from a table, whereas an unorganised listing will reveal no such information.

The principles can be seen from the following table of debtors of a Midlands based company operating through branches in the North and South of England. Accounting records for all branches are kept at head office. The information could have been presented as a simple listing of amounts outstanding from each customer, but would have been very uninformative.

Debtors Outstanding, 31st December 19-1

Period Outstanding	North £	%	Midlands £	%	South £	%	Total £	%
Up to 1 month	69 040	50	83 720	52	21 557	23	174 317	44
Up to 2 months	42 163	30	45 061	28	38 314	42	125 538	32
Up to 3 months	12 647	9	15 038	9	19 713	21	47 398	12
Up to 6 months	8 421	6	12 165	8	9 134	10	29 720	8
Up to 9 months	6 176	5	3 638	2	2 789	3	12 603	3
Up to 12 months	—	—	620	1	797	1	1 417	1
Over 12 months	321	—	—	—	—	—	321	—
Total	138 768	100	160 242	100	92 304	100	391 314	100

Percentage of total debtors 35%   41%   24%   100%

Source: Sales ledger balances, 31st December 19-1

The table shows the total debts outstanding, according to age, for the whole company, together with the percentage that each age band bears to the overall debt. The same information is also shown for each of the branches. From this can be seen several areas for further investigation.

(a) There appears to have been a considerable drop in monthly sales in the South during the latest month.
(b) The payment record in the South seems to lag behind the Midlands and North.
(c) There is a handful of very old debtors in each area, outstanding for more than nine months, which should be investigated immediately. The reason may be disputed deliveries, or simply bad payment on the part of the customer. Whichever is the correct reason, the problem should have been resolved long ago.

A table gives a much more readily understandable presentation of information than a simple listing. It requires some familiarity with figures to understand it properly. To make the presentation easier to understand, visual methods can be used.

Graphs

Spatial relationships are always much easier to see than numerical relationships. A graph aims to present information in the form of a line, or curve, as it is known to statisticians, drawn on squared paper. The detailed figures that are used in a table will be replaced by a visual display, with the objective of showing the general trend of the underlying figures. Impartiality in presentation must be strictly observed, as alterations in the scales used can completely distort the effect. There are other basic rules of graph construction which must be followed in order to obtain an impartial presentation.

(a) A graph is constructed from two variables, one being dependent upon the other, and one which is independent of the other. The independent variable will be recorded on the horizontal axis.

(b) The vertical scale must always start at zero. In order to save space, where the data to be plotted is far from zero, it is permissible to show a break in the scale.

(c) The axes should be labelled clearly to avoid confusion.

(d) The graph must always be given a simple and unambiguous title.

(e) Where two sets of figures are plotted on the same graph, with a large divergence between them, it is usual to record a double vertical scale. Each curve is then read from its own scale.

(f) If there is too much information on the graph, confusion will result. If the curves fall close together, two, or at the most three, curves will be enough to plot. If, however, the curves fall far apart, more can be incorporated without the graph appearing overcrowded.

(g) The source of the figures must be disclosed. The main objective of this type of graph is to present the trend of figures. If detailed figures are required recourse must be had to the original table.

(h) The curves on the graph must be very distinct. The lines must be thick and positive, so that the general upward or

Presentation of Information

downward trend in the figures can be clearly seen. If several curves appear on the graph, they must be distinct to avoid confusion. The use of a continuous line and various broken lines is the best method. This avoids confusion when a graph is photocopied. A key to the curve formation should be included.

(j) A time series graph is one with time plotted along the horizontal axis. When totals are plotted they should be placed at the end of the period to which they relate. Averages should be plotted at the mid-point of the period.

Take the example of a company which operates three production departments, A, B and C. The monthly hours worked by direct labour for the year to 31st December 19-2 in each department are:

19-2	Department A	Department B	Department C	Total
January	1 710	2 500	3 300	7 510
February	1 800	2 440	3 440	7 680
March	1 750	2 610	3 820	8 180
April	1 770	2 330	3 260	7 360
May	1 830	2 700	3 800	8 330
June	1 900	2 680	3 660	8 240
July	1 400	2 000	2 700	6 100
August	1 300	1 800	2 400	5 500
September	1 700	2 550	3 450	7 700
October	1 820	2 690	3 580	8 090
November	1 740	2 500	3 770	8 010
December	1 300	1 750	2 740	5 790
	20 020	28 550	39 920	88 490

From the graph overleaf it can be seen that there are distinct troughs in all departments at Easter, Summer and Christmas, when the works is closed for holidays. Note the use of two different vertical scales, so that the much larger total figures can be included on the same graph.

Histograms

When a frequency distribution is graphed it is known as a histogram. They are often encountered in business life. They are records of the

162 *Accounting for Management*

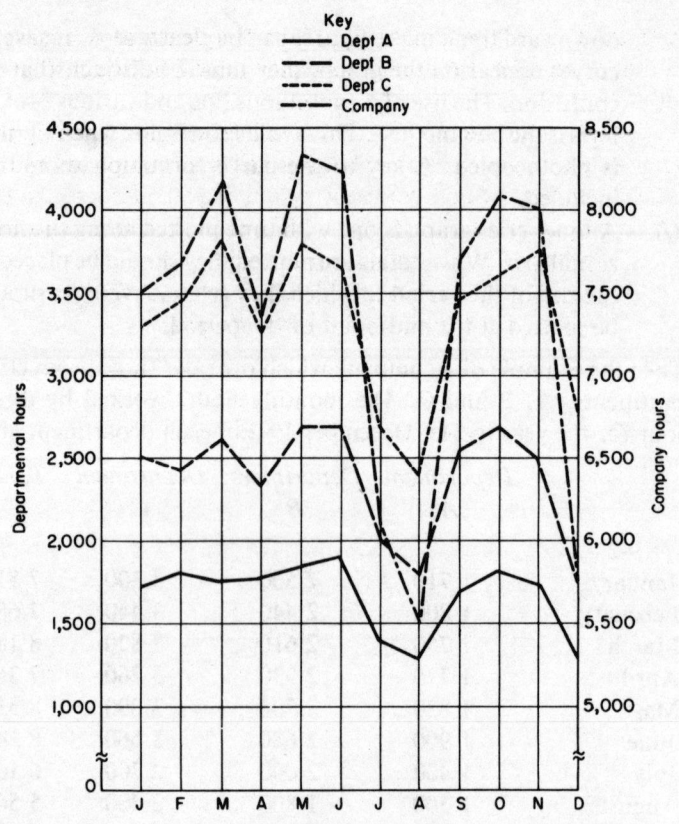

Fig. 16.1 Direct hours worked — departmental and total — year to 31st December 19-2. Source: Production Dept. records

number of times events happen, and can cover all aspects of a business. A large retail chain will graph the takings of its branches each week; a sales manager, — the weekly distance travelled by his representatives; a production manager, — the number of units produced by each direct worker in the department; the despatch manager, — the distance travelled each week by each of his lorries or vans.

A histogram is based upon grouping together all items that fall within a predetermined class. Often the classes are all of equal size. They are plotted along the horizontal axis, and run from one extreme of the distribution to the other. Each class follows on from the previous one, and there are no gaps between classes. The vertical axis is used to plot the frequency, thus forming rectangles. As the size of each class is constant, the area of each rectangle will be in proportion to the frequency of the happening. If the frequency of one class is twice that of another, the area of its rectangle will be double that of the other.

The first stage in the construction of a histogram is to group the frequency distribution. Assume that this has been completed by the sales manager of a national company employing 50 salespersons. He wishes to prepare a histogram of the kilometres travelled in a week by his salespersons. The distribution will be:

Kilometres	Frequency
700 to under 750	4
750 to under 800	7
800 to under 850	20
850 to under 900	11
900 to under 950	8
	50

The histogram will appear as in Fig. 16.2.

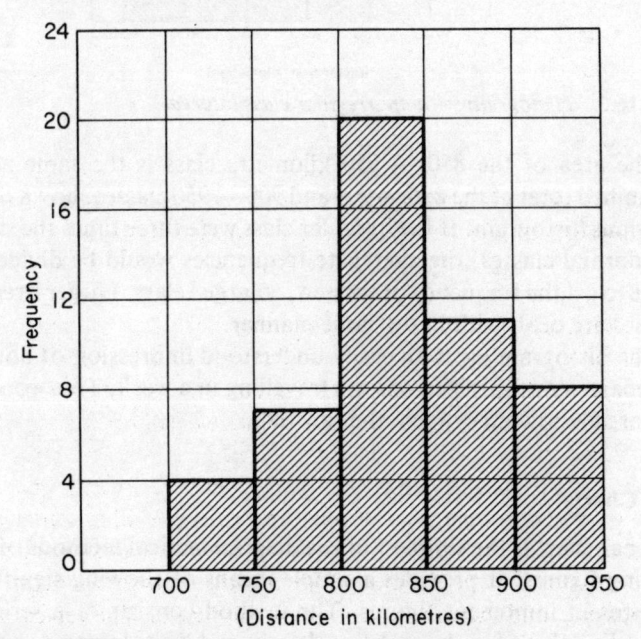

Fig. 16.2 *Histogram of representatives' travelling. Source: returns to sales manager*

If there were an unequal class division, the area of the larger class should be kept in proportion to the other classes. This is achieved by reducing the frequency in line with the increase in class size. If, in the above example, the last two classes were merged, the frequency would be $\frac{19}{2}$ or 9½. The histogram would then appear as in Fig. 16.3, the details being the same as in the previous example.

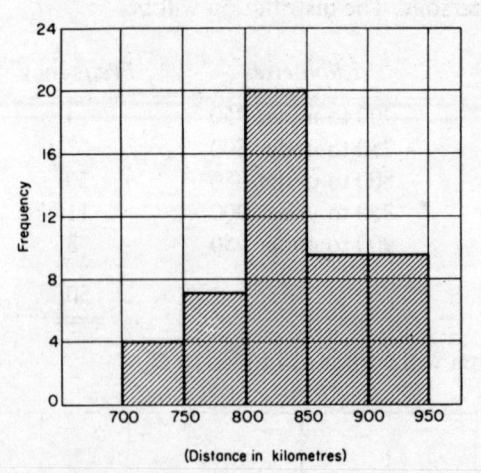

Fig. 16.3 *Histogram with an irregular class interval*

The area of the 850 — 950 kilometre class is the same as the combined total of the 850 — 900 and 900 — 950 classes shown on the previous histogram. If the irregular class were three times the size of the normal classes, the aggregate frequencies would be divided by three to get the frequency of the new, enlarged class. Larger irregular classes are dealt with in the same manner.

The histogram gives an easily understood impression of how far the majority of salespersons are travelling in a week. This would be impossible to convey from the raw data.

Bar Charts

The bar chart is the simplest of the diagrammatical methods of presenting figures. It provides a simple means of showing significant changes in important figures. The method consists of a series of bars, the value of each one being determined by its length or height. The value of each bar may be recorded on it. Alternatively the bars may rest on a horizontal axis representing time, with the vertical axis

Presentation of Information 165

representing a value scale. From this the value of each bar can be ascertained. In this it is very similar to a graph, but there must never be a break to zero on the vertical scale.

Bar charts are a popular method of presenting information about sales to shareholders in company annual reports. Let us use, as an example, the annual sales of Aybecee Ltd for the years 19-0 to 19-4. The company sells three products, A, B and C, and the analysis is shown in the following table.

Sales of Aybecee Ltd, 19-0 to 19-4
analysed by product

	19-0 £'000	%	19-1 £'000	%	19-2 £'000	%	19-3 £'000	%	19-4 £'000	%
Product A	300	25	800	47	900	43	1 000	37	1 300	41
Product B	500	42	600	35	700	33	1 000	37	1 100	34
Product C	400	33	300	18	500	24	700	26	800	25
	1 200	100	1 700	100	2 100	100	2 700	100	3 200	100

Source: Sales office records

The charts may be of four types.

(*a*) **Simple Bar Chart**

This is the simplest form of bar chart in which totals are compared with each other. There is no attempt to compare anything other than the totals.

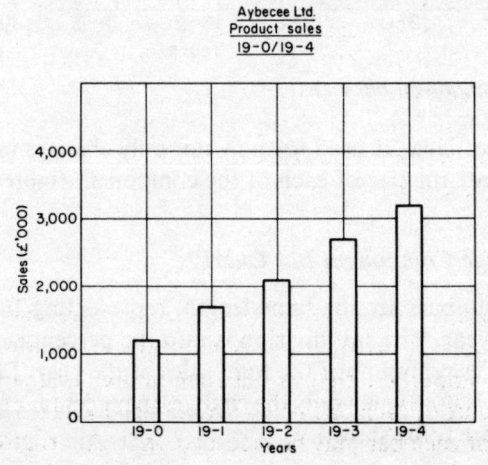

Fig. 16.4 *Simple bar chart*

(b) Actual Component Bar Charts

These are similar to simple bar charts except that the bars are divided into sections. In this case the subdivision is between the sales of each of the three products, according to sales value (Fig. 16.5).

Aybecee Ltd.
Product sales
19-0/19-4

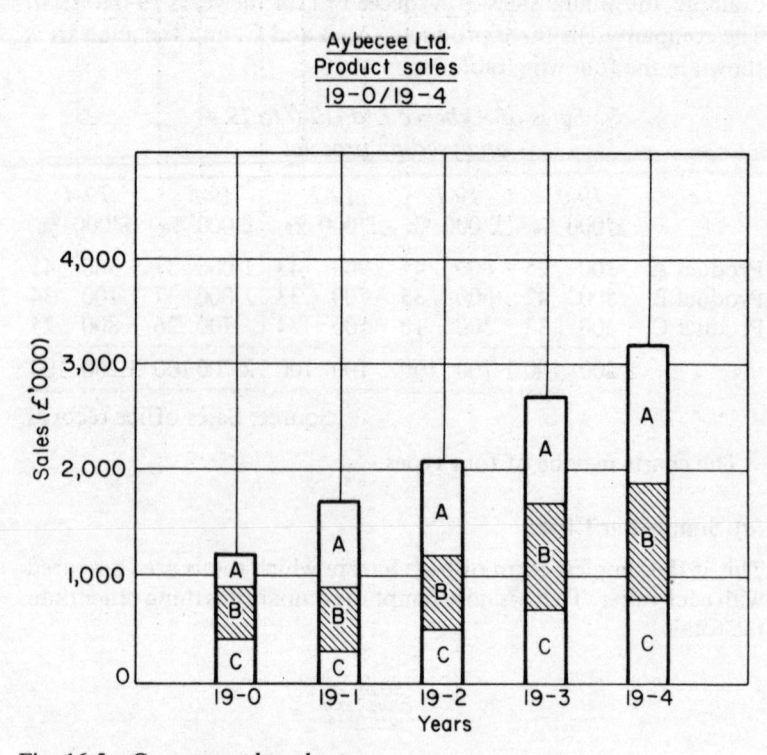

Fig. 16.5 *Component bar chart*

This type of chart is used to show not only changes in total, but also to indicate the size of each of the component figures.

(c) Percentage Component Bar Charts

In this case all bars are the same length, representing 100% of the sales of the year. The sub-division is into the percentage that each product's sales represent of the total sales of the year (Fig. 16.6).

This chart is used when only the changes in percentage size of each component are to be shown.

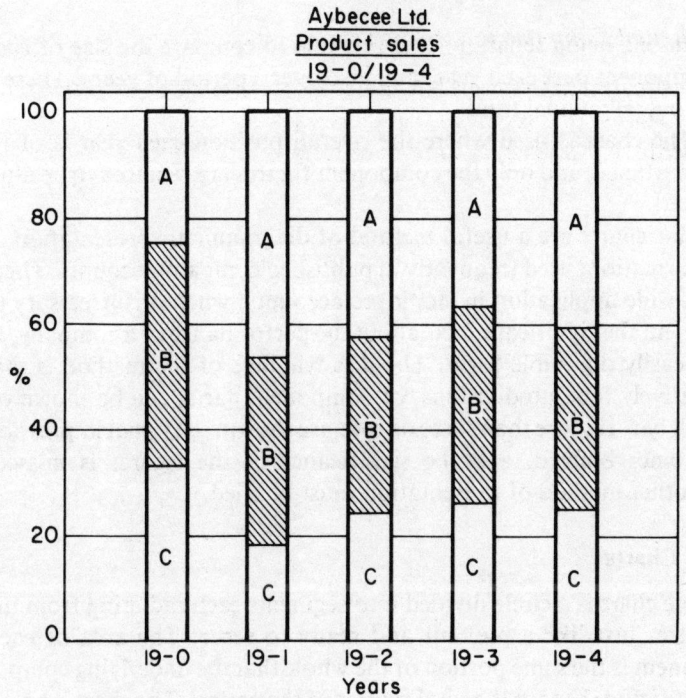

Fig. 16.6 *Percentage bar chart*

(d) Multiple Bar Charts

In these charts only the sizes of the component figures are shown,

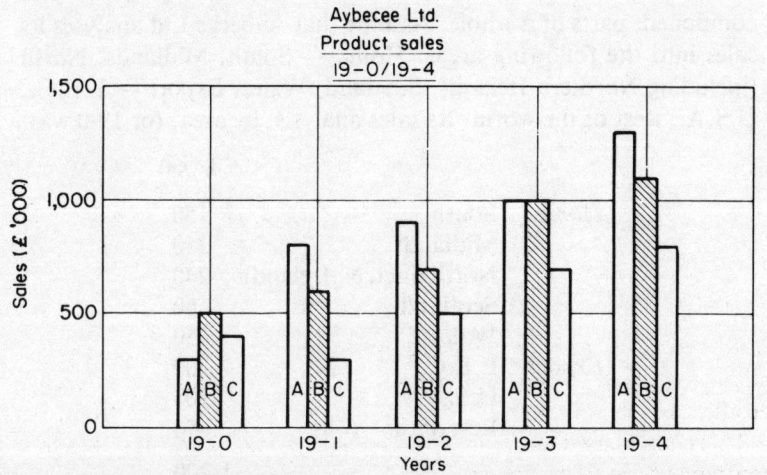

Fig. 16.7 *Multiple bar chart*

each one being separate. It is possible to compare the size of each component part each year, and also over a period of years. There is no overall annual total.

The chart is used where the overall position each year is of no importance, and only the component figures are required to be illustrated.

Bar charts are a useful method of diagrammatic presentation of information, used frequently in published company accounts. There is a wide application in employee accounts, when it is necessary to present the significant facts about the performance of a company, in an easily digestible form. The disadvantage of the method is that relatively few sub-divisions, or component parts, can be shown on each bar. If more than three or four are shown, the visual impression becomes blurred, and the significance of the figures is missed. Another method of presentation must be tried.

Pie Charts

A pie chart is a circle divided into segments each radiating from the centre, just like a pie, cut and ready to serve. The area of each segment is the same portion of the whole that the underlying component figures bear to the total figures of the period. The chart is based upon the fact that the angles in a circle total 360 degrees. The degrees are then split between the component parts of the total figures, proportionately to size. The method can be used, with success, where it is necessary to show the relationship to each other of the several component parts of a whole. Assume that Aybecee Ltd analyses its sales into the following areas: Home — South, Midlands, North (including Northern Ireland), Scotland, Wales; Export — E.E.C., U.S.A., Rest of the world. Its sales analysis, by area, for 19-0 was:

		£'000
Home	South	150
	Midlands	350
	North (incl. N. Ireland)	240
	Scotland	60
	Wales	50
Export	E.E.C.	200
	U.S.A.	100
	Rest of the world	50
		1 200

Presentation of Information 169

360 degrees must now be allocated between the areas in proportion to the sales. The South of England, for example, will be allocated

$$\frac{150}{1\,200} \times 360 = 45°$$

The full allocation is:

		Sales £'000	Degrees
Home	South	150	45
	Midlands	350	105
	North (incl. N. Ireland)	240	72
	Scotland	60	18
	Wales	50	15
Export	E.E.C.	200	60
	U.S.A.	100	30
	Rest of the world	50	15
		1 200	360

Aybecee Ltd.

Midlands £350

South £150

Rest of World £50

U.S.A. £100

E.E.C £200

Wales £50

Scotland £60

North and Northern Ireland £240

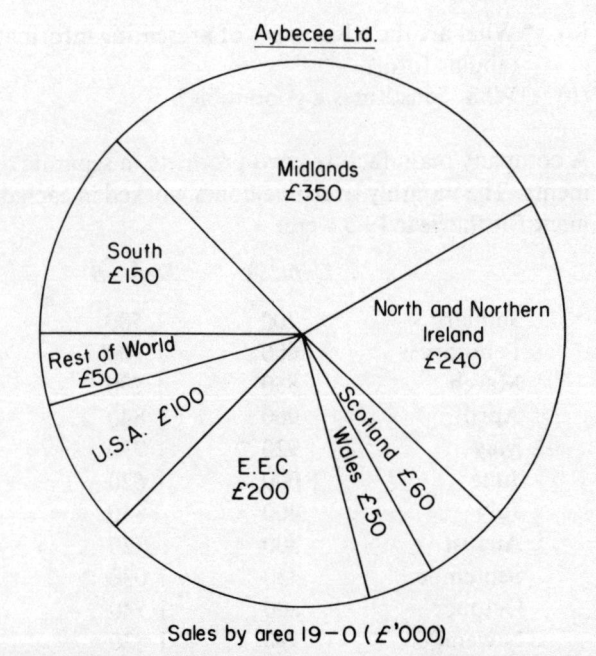

Sales by area 19−0 (£'000)

Fig. 16.8 *Pie chart*

Plot the angles from the centre of a circle and construct the segments, using a compass and a protractor.

Pie charts can be used to illustrate component analyses up to a maximum of about eight. Thereafter the segments can become too small to be effective. The application is not suitable for comparisons covering a series of figures. A series of different pie charts is difficult to compare. Any attempt to convey a visual impression through different sized pie charts will not be successful.

Each year, a limited company is obliged to issue its accounts to all shareholders, at least three weeks before its annual general meeting. In many of the larger companies, special, simplified employee accounts are prepared, explaining in simple terms how the business has fared in the past year. Graphical and diagrammatical presentation is an ideal method of showing some of the information. It has an immediate impact upon people who have no background knowledge of accountancy.

Assignments

16.1. (a) What are the advantages of presenting information in tabular form?
(b) What constitutes a good table?

16.2. A company manufactures two products in separate departments. The monthly overtime hours worked in each department for the year 19-5 were:

	Dept. A	Dept. B
January	700	1 500
February	680	1 700
March	850	1 790
April	900	1 840
May	920	1 730
June	1 000	1 620
July	400	830
August	300	720
September	750	1 030
October	800	1 740
November	990	1 820
December	540	1 310

Presentation of Information 171

Construct a graph to show:

(a) The overtime of each department.
(b) The company overtime for the year 19-5.

16.3. You are the financial controller of a company operating a chain of 98 retail tobacconist shops. The monthly sales of the shops have been grouped together in the following table.

Sales £		Frequency
2 000 to under 2 500		6
2 500	3 000	20
3 000	3 500	28
3 500	4 000	37
4 000	5 000	7
		98

Construct a histogram to show this information.

16.4. Your company is preparing its first set of employee accounts, and is presenting some of the information in diagrammatic form. Present the following information in the most suitable manner.

(a) Home and export sales for the five years 19-2 to 19-6.

	19-2		19-3		19-4		19-5		19-6	
	£'000	%	£'000	%	£'000	%	£'000	%	£'000	%
Home	1 700	68	2 200	65	2 500	57	2 700	53	3 000	49
Export	800	32	1 200	35	1 900	43	2 400	47	3 100	51
	2 500	100	3 400	100	4 400	100	5 100	100	3 100	100

(b) A breakdown of the way in which every £1 of sales income was spent in the year 19-6.

	£
Materials and services	0.30
Wages and salaries	0.34
Interest on borrowings	0.07
Corporation Tax	0.12
Dividends to shareholders	0.02
Retained in the business for future expansion	0.15
	1.00

Explain why you have chosen each method of presentation.

16.5. There are several types of bar chart.

(a) When would you use each of them?
(b) What are the merits and disadvantages of this type of presentation of information?

Answers to Numerical Questions

Part IV
Inflation Accounting

17. Indices

The world has rarely been free from the problems of inflation, and the present period is no exception. Although there have been periods in British history when inflation was severe — notably following the Black Death in 1349, during the Tudor period, and during periods of major warfare — it is only in recent years that the business community has become fully aware of the distorting effects that inflation can have on the accounts of a business. Throughout the centuries accounting has always been based upon the principle of historical cost — goods, services, assets, liabilities and incomes all being recorded at their cost to the business. Where inflation is only a matter of one or two percent a year, it has little effect upon the accuracy of the accounts. As it increases in severity, its effect becomes greater. Ultimately the accounts cease to provide a correct view of the profit for a period, or the financial position of the business at the end of its accounting year. The time has then arrived to adjust the accounts in line with the fall in the purchasing value of money. A statistical technique that is of much assistance in this task is the index number.

What is an index?

It is a technique which makes it possible to compare several series of figures which may be so complex, that any attempt at direct comparison could prove to be meaningless. Take as an example a company manufacturing seven different products. Information is known, over a period of several years, about the individual selling prices of the products, and the numbers of each product manufactured. It is difficult, however, to say which year has the greatest overall production. It is much easier to take a specific year as a base, and express the production of other years as a percentage of this. If 19-0 is taken as the base year and given the number 100, and 19-3 is calculated as 120, it is simple to see that the production of 19-3 is 20% above that of 19-0. The single figure that summarises a whole range of data, and can be used as a basis of comparison with other years, is known as an index number.

The base year mentioned above is the year chosen for comparison with all other years. Most base years are given the figure of 100, analogous to its use in percentages, a concept with which most people are familiar. The index is then expressed as a percentage of that base year. If the average wage paid to a work force in the base year were £70 per week, and the index of wages has now risen to 120, the average wage now should be

$$£70 \times \frac{120}{100} = £84.$$

Index numbers may be of two types:

(a) One item indices.
(b) Multi-item indices.

Within each category two separate indices can be calculated.

(i) The quantity index in which the current year's quantities (q_1) are divided by the base-year quantities (q_0) and multiplied by 100. The formula is:

$$\frac{q_1}{q_0} \times 100.$$

(ii) The price index where the current year's cost or price (p_1) is divided by the base year's cost or price (p_0) and multiplied by 100. The formula is:

$$\frac{p_1}{p_0} \times 100$$

(a) One item indices

The calculation is simple where only one item has to be compared between different periods. A base year is chosen, and the values in the other years are calculated in proportion to the base year values. The following example will illustrate this.

An aluminium gravity die foundry has recorded the following usage of aluminium ingot during a four year period:

	Weight tonnes	Price per tonne £
19-1	24 300	700
19-2	26 000	777
19-3	26 900	833
19-4	28 700	896

Quantity index

		Index
19-1	Base year	100
19-2	$\dfrac{26\ 000}{24\ 300} \times 100$	107
19-3	$\dfrac{26\ 900}{24\ 300} \times 100$	111
19-4	$\dfrac{28\ 700}{24\ 300} \times 100$	118

Price index

		Index
19-1	Base year	100
19-2	$\dfrac{777}{700} \times 100$	111
19-3	$\dfrac{833}{700} \times 100$	119
19-4	$\dfrac{896}{700} \times 100$	128

(*b*) *Multi-item indices*

Indices are usually required in circumstances where there are several items involved. The example used above would apply to a foundry using only one type of aluminium alloy. Most foundries use several types of alloy, or even several types of metal. These metals do not all vary in price in the same proportions. This can be illustrated from the case of a foundry using aluminium, copper and brass and in addition purchasing machined parts which are inserted into the castings. Two major problems now emerge.

(i) The prices of the different metals will move independently of each other. The index will be a compromise of all these movements.
(ii) Although the metals will all be purchased in tonnes, the machined parts will be purchased as a quantity of units. It is obviously not possible to add together tonnes of metal and numbers of machined parts.

Weighting

The problem is overcome by weighting. It is a method of adjusting the value of each item to be included in the index according to its overall importance. The least important item may be brass, followed by machined parts which are twice as important. Copper is three times as important as machined parts, and aluminium is five times as important as copper. The weightings will be:

Brass	1 times
Machined parts	2 times
Copper	6 times
Aluminium	30 times

It is now possible to calculate a weighted price index. The basic information is:

	19-1 Price per tonne £	19-5 Price per tonne £
Aluminium	700	900
Copper	1 900	1 700
Brass	1 400	1 300
Machined parts	500(per 1000)	800(per 1000)

The method consists of the following stages.

(a) Listing the items and their unit costs.
(b) Choosing the appropriate weightings.
(c) Multiplying unit costs by the chosen weightings.

(d) Adding the products together.
(e) Comparing the current year with the base year by calculating the percentage that current year bears to base year.

In statistical terms, the formula for this weighted aggregative index is

$$\frac{\Sigma(p_1 \times w)}{\Sigma(p_0 \times w)} \times 100$$

In everyday language it is:

$$\frac{\text{Price in the current year} \times \text{Weighting}}{\text{Price in the base year} \times \text{Weighting}} \times 100$$

Item	Weighting	Price	Price Weight 19-1	Price	Price Weight 19-5
Brass	1	1 400	1 400	1 300	1 300
Machined Parts	2	500	1 000	800	1 600
Copper	6	1 900	11 400	1 700	10 200
Aluminium	30	700	21 000	900	27 000
			34 800		40 100

The index number for 19-5 if 19-1 is the base year (100) will be:

$$\frac{40\ 100}{34\ 800} \times 100 = \underline{\underline{115}}$$

The method has successfully overcome the problems of different types of material — tonnes and units — and also those of increasing and decreasing costs during the same period. All is reduced to one simple number.

Laspeyre and Paasche Indices

The question of choosing a logical basis of weighting is often overcome by using the actual quantities consumed of each material. This automatically adjusts for importance, as the least used items will form a small part of the whole. This method will give a quantity weighted index. A further problem is then faced. Which quantities

should be used? Those used in the base year, or those used in the current year for which an index is sought?
Both methods are acceptable.

(a) *Base-year quantities* This is known as a Laspeyre index. It is calculated by multiplying the present year price by the base year quantities; dividing by the base year price multiplied by the base year quantities; and multiplying the whole by 100. The formula is:

$$\frac{\Sigma p_1 q_0}{\Sigma p_0 q_0} \times 100$$

(b) *Current-year quantities* This is called a Paasche index, and is calculated by multiplying present year quantities by present year prices; dividing by present year quantities multiplied by base year prices; and multiplying by 100. This formula is:

$$\frac{\Sigma p_1 q_1}{\Sigma p_0 q_1} \times 100$$

The differences between the two methods can be seen by preparing Laspeyre and Paasche indices from the following data:

Item	Price(p_0) £	Quantity(q_0)	Price(p_1) £	Quantity(q_1)
Aluminium (tonnes)	700	30 000	900	40 000
Copper (tonnes)	1 900	400	1 700	500
Brass (tonnes)	1 400	100	1 300	150
Machined parts (thousands)	500	200	800	250

Laspeyre Index	p_0	p_1	q_0	$p_0 \times q_0$	$p_1 \times q_0$
	£	£		£'000	£'000
Aluminium	700	900	30 000	21 000	27 000
Copper	1 900	1 700	400	760	680
Brass	1 400	1 300	100	140	130
Machined parts	500	800	200	100	160
				22 000	27 970

The Laspeyre index is $\dfrac{27\ 970}{22\ 000} \times 100 = \underline{127}$

Paasche Index

	p_0	p_1	q_1	$p_0 \times q_1$	$p_1 \times q_1$
	£	£		£'000	£'000
Aluminium	700	900	40 000	28 000	36 000
Copper	1 900	1 700	500	950	850
Brass	1 400	1 300	150	210	195
Machined parts	500	800	250	125	200
				29 285	37 245

The Paasche index is $\dfrac{37\ 245}{29\ 285} \times 100 = \underline{127}$

Both of the indices give virtually the same figure, but there are fundamental differences in their method of calculation.

(i) With the Laspeyre index the only quantities required are those of the base year. The Paasche index requires quantities for every year. Quantities are more difficult to arrive at than price changes. Only a fundamental change in the relative quantities of materials used will cause a divergence between the two indices. If there is no such change, the Laspeyre index is chosen as being the easier one to calculate.

(ii) The Laspeyre index has a constant denominator which makes it possible to compare each year's index with any other in the series. The Paasche index, with its changing denominator, can only be compared with the base year.

On both these points the Laspeyre index has advantages, and is the one more commonly used.

Availability of Statistics

Every business can build up statistics about its own performance, but there are two main external sources of national and international statistics.

(*a*) *Private sources* Much data is collected and prepared for publication following private investigations. Universities and polytechnics, research bodies, trade unions, political parties, banks and other City institutions, trade associations, building societies — all have their own research departments, which are constantly producing data on various aspects of business life.

(b) *Official sources* The other source, and by far the more important, is known as official statistics. These originate in government departments, and form the basis of the economic policy of the country. Population statistics have been kept for many years. The first national census was held in 1801, and apart from wartime, has been held every decade since. The first census of production was held in 1907, and since the 1950s there has been a three tier structure whereby the Government has kept its finger on the pulse of industry.

(i) Every five years there is a detailed census of all businesses.
(ii) Each year there are less detailed surveys.
(iii) Quarterly, or monthly, there are brief surveys of a sample of firms, which give an indication of the short-term movements in the economy.

The whole of the Government's statistical operation is controlled through the Central Statistical Office which was established in 1941, and the more recent Business Statistics Office situated at Newport, Gwent. A whole range of indices is maintained, such as industrial production, retail sales volume, effective exchange rate for the £, retail prices and average earnings, all of which are published monthly. The index of gross domestic product is published quarterly. In addition there is a host of other subsidiary indices, kept for different industries and trades.

In the international field there are statistics being collected and issued by the international organisations such as the United Nations Organisation and the European Economic Community.

Government statistics are of vital importance in monitoring the position of inflation in the country, and form the basis of schemes that have been suggested for inflation accounting.

Assignments

17.1. Ivor Pitt has obtained a licence from the National Coal Board to work a small drift mine. During his first five years of operation he has recorded his production in tonnes, and average selling price.

	Production (Tonnes)	Average selling price per tonne £
19-4	9 700	20
19-5	11 400	24
19-6	12 900	27
19-7	15 300	31
19-8	18 100	37

REQUIRED:

Prepare quantity and price indices using 19-4 as the base year.

17.2. (i) Why is it necessary to use weightings when preparing a multi-item index?

(ii) Alpha-Beta manufacture three distinct products. The selling price of each product over a five year period was:

Product

	A £	B £	C £
19-6	10.00	5.20	1.10
19-7	11.10	5.90	1.40
19-8	12.20	6.10	1.50
19-9	13.70	7.30	1.90
19-0	14.90	8.10	2.00

The relative importance of each product is

- A 2 times
- B 1 times
- C ½ times

Calculate a weighted aggregative index, using 19-6 as the base period.

17.3. (i) What is the difference between Laspeyre and Paasche indices?

(ii) Which would you recommend in practice, and why?

(iii) The materials purchases for Hurricane Fans Ltd for the three years 19-7 to 19-9 were:

	19-7 Quantity	19-7 Price £	19-8 Quantity	19-8 Price £	19-9 Quantity	19-9 Price £
Sheet Steel (tonnes)	4 500	300	5 400	350	6 000	400
Bar Steel (tonnes)	3 900	480	4 600	510	5 500	550
Electric Motors (units)	15 000	50	16 000	54	17 000	62
Bearings (units)	30 000	10	32 000	11	34 000	12

Prepare Laspeyre and Paasche indices for the three years, using 19-7 as the base year.

18. Adjusting for Inflation

The ravages of inflation are all about us. Over the last fifty years there has been an increase of more than thirty times in the price of property. The average wage in this country has increased eight-fold in the past twenty-five years. The price of petrol has more than quadrupled in the last five years. The value of all these items has not really increased over the years. That which has altered so drastically is the value of the money in which we express the worth of the material aspects of life.

Changes in the Value of Money

The impact of changes in the value of money have had just as great an effect upon business affairs, as they have had upon the everyday life of the populace. There has been a much greater growth in the supply of money than there has been in productivity. The available wealth is represented by far more money than in the past. The position is rather similar to that of a company having an issued share capital of 1 000 000 ordinary shares, with an asset backing of £2 000 000. Each share is worth £2. It decides to capitalise reserves and issue a further 1 000 000 ordinary shares, which are given to shareholders in proportion to their existing shareholdings. The result is that every shareholder now owns two shares, instead of the one held before, but the value of the company has not increased; it is still only worth £2 000 000. The value of each share will, in consequence, drop from £2 to £1. A similar thing is happening to our currency. The more paper money we issue, without the backing of increased creation of wealth, the lower its value falls.

In a business, some assets are being renewed continually. Stock is being converted into debtors daily. It is constantly being replaced by new stock at higher, inflated prices. The result is that the value of stock gradually rises with inflation. Debtors are continually paying their debts in the form of cash, to be replaced by other debts which will be increased by the effect of rising selling prices, forced up by inflation.

As the cost of goods increases, the value of creditors rises. As debtors pay their higher debts, more money becomes available to pay the higher creditors. The cash, stock, debtors and creditors form the elements of working capital in a business. They are the assets and liabilities that are continually changing as a business operates. On the surface the impact of inflation appears small, as there is a constant updating of values as inflation progresses. Below the surface, there are several aspects that give cause for concern.

(a) *Cost of Sales* Where stock is extensive and the rate of inflation is high, the values that are charged into cost of sales can be misleading. If stock records are maintained on a F.I.F.O. basis, the effect will be to charge first into production the longest-held stock. This means that costs will be under-stated in terms of replacement values. The cheaper, older stock values, which are issued to production, must be replaced by more expensive new stock. This can give rise to a two-fold effect:

(i) If management is basing its selling prices upon cost plus a profit margin, it will not attempt to raise those selling prices until the higher-priced stores have worked their way through the system and into production. Failure to act earlier will have sacrificed profit that could otherwise have been made.

(ii) If the company is much more alert it may raise its selling prices as soon as price increases are notified by suppliers. The combination of higher selling prices and low material costs will give an apparently high profit. But how good is that profit when a higher price has to be paid to replace the goods that have been sold?

(b) *Fixed Assets* In the case of fixed assets, the effect of inflation is much more worrying. Once a building or an item of equipment has been bought and posted to an asset account, it remains fixed in the business for many years. The only contact between these assets and the revenue accounts is the annual charge for depreciation, and this is based upon the cost paid for the asset on acquisition. Depreciation is only intended to write down the historical cost of an asset over its useful life. Value equivalent to the original cost of the asset is then retained somewhere in the business. In an inflationary situation, when replacement is needed, the cost is often many times that of the original asset. This gives rise to two major problems.

(i) Depreciation policy will have retained too little value in the business to replace the asset. The low depreciation in the past will have resulted in a higher net profit being shown each year. This profit will have been available for:

  (a) Satisfying the needs of the taxman;
  (b) Paying dividends to shareholders;
  (c) Retention in the business to finance future expansion.

The taxman, in all cases, will take his statutory percentage of the available profit. If the remaining profit is good, the shareholders will expect the highest possible increase in dividends. The remainder will be left in the business for expansion — including the replacement of assets.

(ii) The higher cost of replacing the fixed assets must be found out of retained earnings in the business. If they are insufficient, the business must borrow from the bank manager, or raise additional long-term or permanent capital.

(c) *Fixed-Interest Loans* Another aspect of the business which has been affected by inflation is that of fixed-interest loans. These are often repayable at face value. If the business has invested surplus funds in long-dated, fixed-interest stock, it will be repaid in depreciated value money. The converse applies where the business has issued loan or debenture stocks in the past, and will be redeeming them in the future, with depreciated currency. In the former case a monetary loss will be suffered. In the latter case, a monetary gain will be made. Similar factors apply to debtors and creditors, which both represent a fixed value redeemable in a short period of time, usually no more than two or three months.

Historical Cost and Inflation-Adjusted Accounts

Historical cost accounts do not cater for the problems of inflation. They are based upon the actual cost of assets, costs and services at the time that they are acquired. No attempt is made to adjust for increased replacement costs of stock, and especially fixed assets, even though it is known that prices are soaring. The accountancy profession is, therefore, attempting to alter the form of accounts, in order to illustrate, as far as is possible, the effects of inflation upon the activities of a business.

(*a*) The first move came in May 1974, when the accountancy bodies issued *Statement of Standard Accounting Practice No.* 7, in which was proposed *current purchasing power* (C.P.P.) accounting as a method of adjusting accounts for inflation. The method was based upon updating accounts for changes in general price levels only.

(*b*) In September 1975 an Inflation Accounting Committee, set up by H.M. Government, and known as the Sandilands Committee, made its recommendations. It supported a *current cost accounting* (C.C.A.) approch, in which there would be adjustments to depreciation charges and historical cost of current assets to take into consideration the higher replacement costs of assets.

(*c*) In November 1976 the accountancy bodies issued *Exposure Draft No.* 18, based upon the Sandilands Report and *S.S.A.P.* 7. It supported an alteration in the form of the accounts to adjust for the effects of inflation. Some members of the accountancy profession voted to reject this scheme, on the basis that it would cause confusion if historical cost accounts were abandoned in favour of a system that would difficult to implement.

(*d*) In April 1979 a new *Exposure Draft No.* 24 was issued, in an attempt to get agreement amongst accountants on the best methods of tackling the problem of inflation. It is a compromise solution, whereby historical cost accounts will remain, while a supplementary statement will show the effects of inflation upon the business.

All the methods make extensive use of indices in adjusting for the effects of inflation. The general effects of inflation can be adjusted by applying the Retail Price Index, an index which monitors the price variations of a range of consumer products, and provides a good barometer of general inflation. This method was suggested under the C.P.P. proposals.

With C.C.A. only specific price increases are adjusted, while general price level changes are ignored. While prices will rise at varying rates in different industries, it will be necessary to calculate separate indices for each industry. Large companies could calculate their own indices from their purchase records.

The debate continues. Urgent attempts are being made to get agreement on an acceptable method. The latest proposals in *Exposure Draft No. 24 (E.D. 24)* indicate that the most likely method to be adopted will be based upon C.C.A. It is a compromise, and there is no guarantee that this will prove to be the ultimate solution. Whereas previous thought required the incorporation of inflation accounting adjustments in the books of account, *E.D.* 24 suggests that a separate statement be prepared, in addition to the historical cost accounts. This statement will show the adjustments to the historical profit or loss, and their effect upon the balance sheet, to adjust for the ravages of inflation. In content also, the system is a compromise between the C.P.P. and C.C.A. methods. The method will at first apply only to companies with a turnover in excess of £5 000 000 per annum. There are an estimated 5 500 such companies in the United Kingdom. Some businesses, such as insurance and property companies, are exempt from the proposals.

Conversion to Current Values

At the present it appears that *E.D.* 24 is the system of inflation accounting that is most likely to be adopted in this country. The debate is, however, far from finished, and there are likely to be further changes before a fully satisfactory system is evolved. The principal adjustments at present suggested are:

(*a*) *Cost of Sales Adjustment* This is based on the replacement cost of the stock sold during the period. It should represent the difference between the charge in the historical cost accounts, and the current replacement cost of the stock.

(*b*) *Depreciation Adjustment* This should represent the difference between the depreciation charge in the historical cost accounts, and the true fall in the value of the fixed assets, as a result of earning revenue during the accounting period.

(*c*) *Monetary Working Capital Adjustment* This represents the value — or charge — to the business arising from the finance of debtors and creditors during the accounting period.

190 Accounting for Management

(d) *Gearing Adjustment* Where part of the capital in a business is supplied by loan stock, it will be repaid, at some time in the future, in depreciated currency. It is held, therefore, that there is no need to adjust for inflation on the part of net assets financed by that loan stock. A proportional reduction is made to the current cost adjustment in the revenue account, and the capital maintenance reserve on the balance sheet.

(e) *Capital Maintenance Reserve* This reserve consists of the variations in the value of fixed assets and stock, over and above that which is included in the historical cost accounts, and the monetary working capital adjustment. From the reserve is deducted the gearing adjustment, which reflects the amount of the increases that refer to the finance not provided by shareholders.

Example

The principles involved in preparing an inflation accounting statement under the *E.D.* 24 guidelines can be shown from the following example.

AB Co. Ltd was incorporated on 1st January 19-5, and issued its share capital and purchased its fixed assets at that time. Incomes and expenses are assumed to accrue evenly throughout the year. Closing stocks, debtors and creditors are assumed to relate to the last quarter of the year.

The following price level indices were assumed to exist.

19-5	Average for the year	100
19-8	4th quarter average	160
19-9	Average for the year	180
19-9	4th quarter average	190
19-9	At December 31st	200

The summarised trading and profit and loss account for the year to 31st December 19-9, and the Balance Sheet at that date, prepared on a historic cost basis, were:

Trading and Profit & Loss Account for the year to 31st December 19-9

	£	£
Sales		420 000
Opening stock	50 000	
Add Purchases	300 000	
	350 000	
Less Closing stock	70 000	280 000
Gross profit		140 000
Depreciation	20 000	
Expenses	80 000	100 000
Net profit		£40.000

Balance Sheet at 31st December 19-9

	£
Fixed assets at cost	300 000
Less Depreciation	100 000
	200 000
Stock	70 000
Debtors	90 000
Bank	20 000
	£380 000

Represented by:	£
Issued share capital	200 000
Reserves	50 000
10% debentures	100 000
Creditors	30 000
	£380 000

The indices used for adjustment should be the ones most suitable for the industry. They could well be different for machinery, buildings and stock. In this example, to make the adjustment simpler, it is assumed that the one index applies to all aspects of the business.

The adjustments will be calculated in the following manner.

(a) *Cost of Sales Adjustment* The historical cost profit will have been adjusted by the straight difference between the opening and closing stocks. This created a movement of £70 000 less £50 000, or £20 000. The opening stock was valued at the prices prevailing during the last quarter of 19-8 (index 160) and the closing stock at those prevailing one year later (index 190). Both must be adjusted to the average price prevailing during 19-9 (index 180).

		£
Adjusted closing stock	£70 000 × $\frac{180}{190}$ =	66 316
Adjusted opening stock	£50 000 × $\frac{180}{160}$ =	56 250
Adjusted stock movement		£10 066

The difference between the historic cost and inflation adjusted movements (£20 000 less £10 066) is £9 934, and this will represent the cost of sales adjustment. This amount will be debited in the profit and loss account, thus reducing the profit, and credited to the capital maintenance reserve.

(b) *Fixed Asset and Depreciation Adjustment* The fixed assets were all bought at the time of commencement of the business, when the index stood at 100. Now the index has doubled to 200. The replacement value of those fixed assets will likewise have doubled from £300 000 to £600 000. The depreciation charge for the year 19-9 should be based upon the inflation-adjusted replacement cost of £600 000. Any backlog depreciation, due for previous years, is to be adjusted through a transfer to the capital maintenance reserve. The inflation adjustment is:

	Gross value £	Depreciation £	Net value £
Value at end 19-8	300 000	80 000	220 000
Revaluation including backlog depreciation to 19-8	300 000	80 000	220 000
Depreciation for 19-9 (doubled)		40 000	(40 000)
Value at end of 19-9	£600 000	£200 000	£400 000

The revaluation and backlog depreciation of £220 000 will be adjusted by debiting net fixed assets, and crediting the capital maintenance reserve.

An additional adjustment of £20 000 to cover the extra current cost depreciation is needed. It will be debited in the profit and loss account, and will already have been credited against the fixed asset account in the charge of £40 000.

(c) *Monetary Working Capital Adjustment* This represents an adjustment to the net amount of debtors less creditors arising from recent inflation. We are told, in this example, that debtors and creditors arise during the final quarter of the year, when the index stood at 190. At the end of the year, the index had risen to 200. The current value of net debtors should be:

	£
£90 000 − £30 000 = £60 000 × $\frac{200}{190}$ =	63 158
Less Historic cost value	60 000
Monetary working capital adjustment	3 158

This amount must be debited in the current cost profit and loss account, and credited to the capital maintenance reserve in the balance sheet.

(d) *Gearing Adjustment* At this stage the historic cost profit has been reduced by the following amounts.

	£
Cost of sales adjustment	9 934
Depreciation	20 000
Monetary working capital adjustment	3 155
	£33 089

In the historic cost balance sheet the finance for the company is supplied £250 000 (£200 000 share capital and £50 000 reserves) by shareholders, and £100 000 by debenture stockholders. The debenture holders will be repaid only the face value of their debentures, unaffected by inflation. It is considered to be unnecessary to adjust for the effects of inflation upon those assets which are financed by debentures which are not subject to inflation as far as the business is concerned.

The current cost adjustment is reduced by the proportion that loan capital bears to total loan and share capital i.e. 100 : 350, or 2/7ths. This is called the gearing adjustment, and is calculated:

$$£33\,089 \times \frac{2}{7} = £9\,454$$

This adjustment will be added to the current cost profit in the profit and loss account, and deducted from the capital maintenance reserve on the balance sheet.

(*e*) *Capital Maintenance Reserve* This account appears on the liabilities section of the balance sheet, and represents the amount by which inflation has raised the value of assets in the business, over and above the historic cost. The balance on the account represents the increase in value that belongs to the shareholders, and is reduced by the gearing adjustment.

	£
Cost of sales adjustment	9 934
Monetary working capital adjustment	3 155
Revaluation of fixed assets	220 000
	233 089
Less Gearing adjustment	9 454
	£223 635

The current cost accounting statement can now be prepared.

Current Cost Summarised Profit & Loss Statement for the year to 31st December 19-9

	£	£
Sales		£400 000
Profit per historic cost accounts		40 000

	£	£
Less Current cost adjustments:		
Cost of sales adjustment	9 934	
Monetary working capital adjustment	3 155	
Depreciation	20 000	33 089
		6 911
Add Gearing adjustment		9 454
Current cost profit attributable to shareholders		£16 365

Current Cost Balance Sheet at 31st December 19-9

	£
Assets	
Fixed assets	400 000
Stock	70 000
Debtors *less* Creditors (£90 000 − £30 000)	60 000
Bank	20 000
	£550 000
Represented by:	
Share capital	200 000
Reserves (£10 000 + £16 365)	26 365
Capital maintenance reserve	223 635
	450 000
10% Debentures	100 000
	£550 000

Inflation Adjustments in Later Years

Having set up a system of reporting on the effects of inflation, a similar procedure must be carried out in all later years. The same basic principles will be applied, although there will be slight differences when calculating the depreciation and fixed asset adjustment and the capital maintenance reserve. The method can be illustrated by taking the summarised historic cost accounts for AB Co. Ltd, for the year to 31st December 19-0.

Historic Cost Profit Summary for the year to 31st December 19-0

	£
Sales	500 000
Total costs and expenses	480 000
Net profit	£20 000

Historic Cost Balance Sheet at 31st December 19-0

	£
Assets	
Fixed assets at cost	300 000
Depreciation	120 000
	180 000
Stock	90 000
Debtors *less* Creditors	70 000
Bank	30 000
	£370 000

	£
Represented by:	
Issued share capital	200 000
Reserves	70 000
10% Debentures	100 000
	£370 000

It is assumed that there is no increase in issued share capital or fixed assets during the year. The indices for 19-0 are:

Average for the year	230
4th quarter average	240
At 31st December 19-0	250

In order to prepare inflation adjusted accounts, the appropriate adjustments must first be calculated.

(*a*) *Cost of Sales Adjustment* This will be prepared in exactly the same way as before.

Closing stock	£90 000 ×	$\dfrac{230}{240}$ =	86 250
Opening stock	£70 000 ×	$\dfrac{230}{190}$ =	84 737
			£1 513

Historic cost movement	20 000
Less Current cost movement	1 513
	£18 487

(*b*) *Monetary Working Capital Adjustment* This also is prepared in the same way as before.

Adjusted net debtors	£70 000 ×	$\dfrac{250}{240}$ =	72 917
Less Historic cost net debtors			70 000
			£2 917

(*c*) *Fixed Asset and Depreciation Adjustment* This statement will start with the final figures of the previous year's statement. The revaluation adjustment, including backlog depreciation, will be calculated by applying this year's index at 31st December (250) and last year's index at the same date (200). The depreciation for 19-0 will be based upon the newly adjusted gross cost.

	Gross value £	Depreciation £	Net value £
Value at end of 19-9	600 000	200 000	400 000
Revaluation including backlog depreciation	150 000	50 000	100 000
	750 000	250 000	500 000
Depreciation 19-0		50 000	(50 000)
	£750 000	£300 000	£450 000

(d) *Gearing Adjustment* The total capital invested in the business, as shown by the historic cost balance sheet, is £370 000. The debenture element is still £100 000. The gearing adjustment will be

$$\frac{100}{370} \times \text{Profit and loss adjustment:}$$

	£
Cost of sales adjustment	18 487
Monetary working capital adjustment	2 917
Depreciation	30 000
	£51 404

The gearing adjustment is $\frac{100}{370} \times £51\ 404 = £13\ 893$

(e) *Capital Maintenance Reserve* The balance on this account at the end of 19-9 will be adjusted by the 19-0 entries.

	£	£
Balance forward		223 635
Add Adjustments for 19-0: C.O.S.A.	18 487	
M.W.C.A.	2 917	
Revaluation	100 000	
	121 404	
Less Gearing adjustment	13 893	
		107 511
Balance at 31st December 19-0		£331 146

The revised inflation adjusted statement can now be prepared.

*Current Cost Summarised Profit & Loss Statement
for the year to 31st December 19-0*

	£	£
Sales		£500 000
Historic cost profit		20 000

	£	£
Less Current cost adjustments:		
Cost of sales adjustment	18 487	
Monetary working capital adjustment	2 917	
Depreciation (£50 000 − £20 000)	30 000	51 404
Current cost loss		(31 404)
Less Gearing adjustment		13 893
Current cost loss attributable to shareholders		£(17 511)

Current Cost Balance Sheet at 31st December 19-0

	£
Assets	
Fixed assets	450 000
Stock	90 000
Debtors (net)	70 000
Bank	30 000
	£640 000

	£
Represented by:	
Issued share capital	200 000
Reserves (£26 365 − £17 511)	8 854
Capital maintenance reserve	331 146
	540 000
10% Debentures	100 000
	£640 000

The fundamental principles that have been applied in calculating the current cost accounting statements are:

(*a*) Against the income of the business must be offset the full cost of the assets used in earning that income, based upon current replacement cost.

(*b*) The balance sheet must be adjusted to show the latest

replacement cost of all assets, with the exception of cash.

(c) If any part of the assets are financed by loan capital, repayable in depreciated currency, the adjustment to profit will be reduced, in the proportion that loan capital bears to total capital. There will be no corresponding adjustment to the increased value of assets shown in the balance sheet, as all surpluses on realisation will belong to the ordinary shareholders. Loan stockholders receive back only the face value of their loan.

It is probable that there will be refinements to the technique of adjusting historic-cost accounts for inflation, but it is likely that the above principles will continue to apply.

Assignments

18.1. Why is it necessary to adjust historic cost accounts in a period of inflation?

18.2. Describe briefly the main recent steps to attempt to introduce an acceptable method of inflation accounting.

18.3. What are the main adjustments to historic cost accounts recommended in *Exposure Draft No. 24*?

18.4. Describe, with examples, how you would calculate the following adjustments when preparing a current cost accounting statement;
   (a) Cost of sales adjustment;
   (b) Monetary working capital adjustment;
   (c) Gearing adjustment;
   (d) Depreciation and fixed asset adjustment during the first year of adjusting for the effects of inflation;
   (e) Capital maintenance reserve.

18.5. IP Co. Ltd was formed, and started trading on 1st January 19-2. It issued its share capital on that day, and shortly afterwards purchased its fixed assets. It is assumed that incomes and expenses accrue evenly throughout the year. Closing stocks, debtors and creditors all relate to the last quarter of the year.

The following general price indices existed:

19-2	Average for the year	150
19-6	4th quarter average	210
19-7	Average for the year	230
19-7	4th quarter average	240
19-7	At December 31st	250

The trading and profit and loss account for the year to 31st December 19-7, and the balance sheet at that date, prepared on a historic cost basis, were:

Summarised Profit & Loss Account for the year to 31st December 19-7

	£'000	£'000
Sales		6 000
Opening stock	700	
Purchases	4 000	
	4 700	
Less Closing stock	800	3 900
Gross profit		2 100
Depreciation	400	
Expenses	1 500	1 900
Net profit		£ 200

Balance Sheet at 31st December 19-7

	£'000
Fixed assets at cost	4 000
Less Depreciation	2 400
	1 600
Stock	800
Debtors (net of creditors)	600
Bank	200
	3 200

	£'000
Financed by:	
Issued share capital	2 300
Reserves	900
	3 200

REQUIRED Prepare a current cost statement for the first time for this business, incorporating:

(*a*) Cost of sales adjustment;
(*b*) Monetary working capital adjustment;
(*c*) Fixed asset and depreciation adjustment;
(*d*) Capital maintenance reserve.

Show your workings.

18.6. At the end of the following year to 31st December 19-8, IP Co. Ltd produced the following historic cost accounts:

Summarised Profit Statement for the year to 31st December 19-8

	£'000
Sales	7 000
Less Costs and expenses	6 900
Net profit	100

Balance Sheet at 31st December 19-8

	£'000
Fixed assets at cost	4 000
Less Depreciation	2 800
	1 200
Stock	1 050
Debtors (net of creditors)	800
Bank	250
	3 300

Represented by:

	£'000
Issued share capital	2 300
Reserves	1 000
	3 300

The indices for 19-8 were:

Average for the year	280
4th quarter average	290
At 31st December 19-8	300

The accounting policies of the previous year remained unchanged, and there were no changes of fixed assets.

REQUIRED: Prepare a current cost statement for the company for the year to 31st December 19-8, following on from that prepared in question 18.5.

18.7. When IP Co. Ltd was formed it was decided to finance the business on the following basis:

	£'000
Issued ordinary shares	1 500
8% Debentures	800
	2 300

Apart from this one change, the accounts were in all other respects exactly as presented in questions 18.5 and 18.6.

REQUIRED:

(a) How will the current cost statement now differ?
(b) Prepare a current cost statement for the year to 31st December 19-7.
(c) Prepare a similar statement for the year to 31st December 19-8.

19. Additional Assignments

19.1. A. Neale commenced business on 1st July 19-1 as a manufacturer of a standard, high-speed drill. The trial balance extracted from his books on 30th June 19-2 contained the following balances:

	£
Purchases of raw materials	59 600
Sales	273 000
Returns outwards	500
Carriage inwards	1 500
Productive wages	59 000
Royalties	9 200
Rent and rates (80% works)	23 500
Power, light and heat (75% works)	10 000
Indirect labour	28 000
Repairs	8 100
Depreciation of plant and machinery	14 100
Consumables	5 500
Telephones and postages	2 100
Stationery	1 400
Salaries	15 000
Depreciation of office equipment	2 200
Travelling and entertainment	4 600
Salesmen's salaries	14 200
Motor expenses	3 100
Depreciation of motor vehicles	2 600

	£
Carriage outwards	6 200
Loan interest	3 300
Discount allowed	800

Sufficient raw material was purchased to produce 101 000 drills, and enough was issued to production departments for the manufacture of 96 000 drills.

At the end of the year, work in progress stock was 100% complete for material, and 50% complete for wages and works overheads.

Royalties are payable at 10p on all drills actually finished, and transferred to finished goods store.

All sales were made at a standard price of £3 per unit.

REQUIRED:

(a) Calculate closing stocks of raw materials, work in progress and finished goods.
(b) Prepare manufacturing, trading and profit and loss accounts for the year to 30th June 19-2.

19.2. PQ Ltd manufacture two products, each in a separate factory, and the following information is available about each one.

Product	A	B
Direct materials per unit	£9	£10
Direct labour per unit	£4	£7
Variable overheads per unit	£5	£5
Selling price per unit	£24	£30
Break-even point, in units	3 200	2 800

REQUIRED:

(a) Prepare a statement showing:
  (i) The marginal unit cost of each product;
  (ii) When 4 000 units of each product are produced, the total marginal cost, fixed cost, total cost and profit for each product.
(b) Each factory produced 3 500 units, of which 3 000 are sold. Prepare a statement showing the costs, stock and

profit for each product. Stock is valued on the basis of marginal cost for product A, and absorption (or total) cost for product B.

(c) Assume that the same type of raw material is used to manufacture both products, and it is in short supply. Each factory has the capacity to more than double production, and customers are clamouring for both products. State which is the better product to manufacture, giving your reasons.

(d) State the arguments for and against the valuation of stock on the basis of:
   (i) Absorption cost;
   (ii) Marginal cost.

19.3. Stanco Ltd manufactures a uniform product. The standard cost of producing 5 000 units is:

| Direct materials | 2 500 kg costing £6 000 |
| Direct labour | 6 250 hours costing £10 000 |

During the month of January 19-3, 5 600 units were produced, the actual cost being:

| Direct materials | 2 900 kg costing £6 815 |
| Direct labour | 6 750 hours costing £11 070 |

REQUIRED:

(a) Report to the managing director on the reasons for discrepancies that arose between standard and actual cost for the month's production, specifying the following variances:
   (i) Labour rate;
   (ii) Labour efficiency;
   (iii) Material price;
   (iv) Material usage.
(b) In what circumstances would the use of a system of standard costing be unsuitable?

19.4. S. White has completed his first year of trading, and produced the following balance sheet at 31st August 19-2:

	£
Fixed assets	8 400
Stock	2 100
Debtors for sales: July	1 200
August	3 000
Bank balance	700
	£15 400

	£
Capital	13 400
Creditors for purchases	1 830
Creditors for expenses	170
	£15 400

His forecasts for the four months to 31st December 19-2 are;

	Sales £	Purchases £	Wages £	Expenses (incl. depreciation) £
September	3 600	2 400	320	600
October	3 900	2 700	350	630
November	4 500	3 600	390	690
December	4 800	3 000	470	720

You are given the following information:

(a) Sales are all on a credit basis, and one third of the debtors pay in the month following sale, and receive a cash discount of 3%. These discounts are not included in the forecast figures. The remainder of the debtors pay in the second month after sale.

(b) 40% of purchases are paid for in the month of delivery, and the remainder in the following month.

(c) One half of all expenses are paid for in cash. The remainder are paid in the following month.

(d) Depreciation of fixed assets is a constant charge of £140 per month.

(e) S. White intends to draw £120 per month from the business.

(f) The value of stock at 31st December 19-2 is expected to be £2 000.
(g) Wages are paid in the month in which they are incurred.

REQUIRED: You have been employed by S. White to:

(a) Prepare a cash budget to show balances at the end of each of the four months September to December 19-2;
(b) Prepare a forecast trading and profit and loss account for the four months to December 19-2, and a balance sheet at that date;
(c) Advise on any urgent action that may be required.

19.5. You are the budget accountant of B. Bouncer, rubber ball manufacturers, and you are unhappy about the budget estimates for the year 19-4, submitted by the sales manager for:

(a) Sales;
(b) Salesmen's commission;
(c) Transport costs.

The following information is available on your files, for the actual results of the past four years.

Sales	1st quarter	2nd quarter	3rd quarter	4th quarter
	£	£	£	£
19-0	100 000	130 000	70 000	150 000
19-1	120 000	160 000	80 000	190 000
19-2	150 000	200 000	90 000	210 000
19-3	180 000	230 000	100 000	240 000

Salesmen's commission	(total for year)
	£
19-0	18 100
19-1	22 100
19-2	24 800
19-3	29 700

Travelling expenses £
19-0	4 100
19-1	5 700
19-2	6 500
19-3	7 800

You establish that there are no exceptional circumstances which will affect results during the budget period.

REQUIRED:

(a) Calculate the estimated trend of quarterly and annual sales for the budget year 19-4 from a time-series graph.
(b) From scatter graphs estimate the budget figures for:
  (i) Salesmen's commissions;
  (ii) Travelling expenses.

19.6. The summarised balance sheets of B. Line Ltd at 31st December 19-3 and 31st December 19-4 were as follows;

	19-3 £	19-4 £
Issued share capital	300 000	400 000
General reserves	80 000	90 000
Profit & loss account balance	58 000	67 000
Proposed dividends	20 000	25 000
Sundry creditors	19 000	24 000
Taxation	15 000	13 000
Bank overdraft	6 200	—
	£498 000	£619 000
Freehold property at cost	175 000	245 000
Machinery at cost	105 000	180 000
Provision for depreciation on machinery	(29 000)	(52 000)
Investments	35 100	20 000
Debtors	89 300	94 000
Stock	122 800	102 000
Bank balance	—	30 000
	£498 200	£619 000

REQUIRED

(a) Prepare a source and application of funds statement to show the changes in the bank balance between the two balance sheet dates.

(b) Show the source and application of funds in a suitable graphical form.

19.7. Ivor Grimethorpe is a self-made man. He set up in business twenty years ago as a small tool merchant, and has since commenced manufacture. His accounts reveal a steady profit rise each year. The stock in the annual accounts is at 'director's valuation', and now forms by far the largest item of current assets.

Ivor has decided, on doctor's advice, to take life more easily, and has appointed you to be his management accountant. You ask to see the stock records, and receive the reply that there has been no need for them, as Mr Grimethorpe can look at the physical stock and estimate the value 'with enough accuracy for the accounts'.

You start a stock investigation and discover that the true value of the stock is £100 000 less than stated in the balance sheet.

REQUIRED: Write a report to Ivor Grimethorpe explaining:

(a) How stock should be valued.
(b) The various methods of keeping stores records.
(c) The effects of the various methods of stock evaluation upon profit.
(d) A method of stock recording and evaluation that you recommend should be adopted in the business, and the effect it will have on the current, and future, years' results.

19.8. The summarised final accounts of Dealers Ltd, a wholesale warehouse, for the two years to 30th September 19-5 and 19-6 were as follows:

Trading and Profit and Loss Accounts

	19-5		19-6	
	£	£	£	£
Sales		500 000		600 000
Less Opening stock	80 000		70 000	
Purchases	340 000		450 000	
	420 000		520 000	
Less				
Closing stock	70 000	350 000	110 000	410 000
Gross profit		150 000		190 000
Administration overheads	85 000		92 000	
Selling and distribution overheads	30 000		40 000	
Finance overheads (loan interest)	5 000	120 000	8 000	140 000
Net profit		30 000		50 000
Proposed ordinary dividend		20 000		30 000
Retained profit		10 000		20 000
Balance forward from last year		70 000		80 000
Balance to balance sheet		£80 000		£100 000

Balance Sheets at 30th September

	19-5		19-6	
	£	£	£	£
Capital employed:				
Issued ordinary share capital (shares of 50p)		200 000		200 000
Profit and loss account		80 000		100 000

212 Accounting for Management

	£	£	£	£
Long-term liabilities		50 000		80 000
		330 000		380 000
Represented by:				
Fixed assets *less* depreciation		230 000		240 000
Debtors	50 000		70 000	
Other current assets	130 000		140 000	
	180 000		210 000	
Less Current liabilities (creditors)	80 000	100 000	70 000	140 000
		£330 000		£380 000

The market value of the shares at each balance sheet date was:

　　　　　　　19-5　£0.55
　　　　　　　19-6　£1.04

REQUIRED:

(*a*) Use ratios to prepare a report evaluating the financial standing of the company in the two years 19-5 and 19-6.

(*b*) How do you rate the company as an investment prospect?

Ignore the effect of taxation.

19.9.　You have recently been appointed management accountant to the Jubilee Fertiliser Co. Ltd, which was founded in 1897. It has maintained a steady profit growth record throughout its history until six years ago. Since then, despite increased sales, profits have been falling.

　　The company has for many years manufactured five types of fertiliser, which are sold to farmers. Sales accrue evenly throughout the year, and you discover that an analysis of sales by product was made six years ago, just before profits started to decline. The details were:

Product	Selling price per tonne £	Tonnage
A	20	4 000
B	24	2 400
C	27	1 700
D	31	1 500
E	18	5 100

The present selling prices for the products are:

Product	£ per tonne
A	65
B	80
C	91
D	89
E	62

At your first management committee meeting, the sales manager requested permission to employ an extra salesman 'to cope with the increased work-load resulting from higher sales during the last six years'. It will be a major task to analyse the current year's sales, and you have to advise the managing director the next day if you consider that the sales manager's request is valid. The sales for the first six months of the current year were £485 000, an estimated rate for the full year of £970 000.

REQUIRED:
(a) Calculate an index which will enable you quickly to determine whether there has been a real, or only apparent, increase in turnover over the past six years.
(b) Does this throw light upon the financial problems of the company?

19.10. You are the financial director of a company which was formed in 19-0. Since then it has made a small profit each year, but no dividend has been paid for the last four years due to major cash shortages.

Accounts have always been prepared on the historic cost basis, for the year to 31st December. During the year 19-9, the profit has been the best for some time, but you have persuaded your fellow directors to recommend that no dividend be paid again, as cash is still in short supply. You have just been informed that a group of major shareholders will be placing a resolution before the annual general meeting recommending that a dividend of 40% be paid on all ordinary shares.

All the fixed assets of the business were bought during the first year of its existence, and they are being depreciated in equal instalments over a period of fifteen years. Incomes and expenses accrue evenly throughout the year, and closing stocks, debtors and creditors all relate to the last quarter of the year.

The following general price indices apply to the business:

19-0	Average for the year	100
19-8	Fourth quarter average	250
19-9	Average for the year	280
19-9	Fourth quarter average	290
19-9	At December 31st	300

The summarised trading and profit and loss accounts for the year to 31st December 19-9 and the balance sheet at that date, prepared on the historic cost basis were:

Trading & Profit & Loss Account

	£'000	£'000
Sales		1 400
Opening stock	300	
Purchases	1 050	
	1 350	
Less Closing stock	400	950
Gross profit		450
Depreciation	40	
Expenses	350	390
Net profit		60

Balance Sheet at 31st December 19-9

		£'000
Fixed assets at cost		600
Less Depreciation		400
		200
Stock		400
Debtors	350	
Less Creditors	120	230
Bank		20
		850
Financed by:		
Issued share capital		700
Reserves		150
		850

REQUIRED: Prepare a current cost statement for submission to the annual general meeting, containing:

(*a*) Cost of sales adjustment;
(*b*) Monetary working capital adjustment;
(*c*) Fixed asset and depreciation adjustments;
(*d*) Capital maintenance reserve.

Show all your workings.

Answers to Numerical Questions

2.2 Prime cost £309 000; Production cost £470 000

2.3 Prime cost £34 700; Production cost £53 000
Gross profit £18 500; Net profit £3 900

2.4 Prime cost £40 640; Manufacturing profit £8 400
Trading profit £19 600; Net profit £12 620

3.3 Stock value £110.25

3.4 Stock value £107.35

3.5 Stock value £109.78

3.6

	June £	December £
FIFO	30.00	110.25
LIFO	30.00	106.50
AVCo	30.00	108.58

3.7

	FIFO £	LIFO £	AVCo £
Gross profit — June	200.00	200.00	200.00
— Dec.	423.25	420.35	422.78

3.8

	FIFO £	LIFO £	AVCo £
Gross profit — June	200.00	200.00	200.00
— Dec.	423.25	419.50	421.58

Answers to Numerical Questions 217

5.1 Total cost £1 004

5.3 Machine shop £9.80 per hour; Electro-plating shop £2.00 per hour; Assembly shop £2.50 per hour

6.2 Equivalent production 24 350 units

6.3

	Finished goods stock £	W.I.P. stock £
19-0	14 000	10 500
19-1	65 000	6 500
19-2	36 000	8 400

6.4 (a) Finished goods £31 520
(b) Profit on sales £9 880

8.5 Variances Material price   £240 (favourable)
              Material usage   £600 (adverse)
              Labour rate   £2 820 (favourable)
              Labour efficiency   £720 (adverse)

9.3 Yes

9.4 Yes

9.5 Approximately £13 200

9.6 (e) Approximate sales: Quarter 1 £320 000; 2 £435 000; 3 £865 000; 4 £300 000

10.3 (a) Yes (b) Yes (c) No (d) No

11.1
Gross profit	£105 000
Net profit	£35 700
Fixed assets	£69 400
Current assets	£97 400
Capital and current accounts	£122 800
Current liabilities	£44 000

11.2 First week of June

11.3 Cash at bank, 30th June   £10 835

11.4
Bank overdraft, 30th June	£12 200
Gross profit	£51 000
Net profit	£33 825

218 *Accounting for Management*

	Fixed assets	£47 025
	Current assets	£84 500
	Capital	£98 725
	Current liabilities	£32 800

13.2 Decrease in cash £15 000
Net decrease in working capital £13 000

13.5 Decrease in cash £114 000
Net decrease in working capital £146 000

14.3 Reject. Loss increases to £4 500 per month.

14.5
	Profit	
	Without works overheads	*Including works overheads*
	£	£
19-7	20 000	26 000
19-8	58 000	55 000
19-9	4 000	3 000

15.3 (*a*) Current ratio 1.53; Acid test ratio 0.84

15.4 £22 000

15.5 (*a*) *Profitability*
Rate of gross profit 24%; Rate of net profit 9%; Return on capital employed 13.7%; Net profit after tax/owners' equity 11.1%
(*b*) *Liquidity*
Current ratio 2.1; Acid test ratio 1.3
(*c*) *Asset usage*
Debtor collection 54.8 days; Stock turnover 8 times; Sales/fixed assets 1.4
(*d*) *Capital structure*
Fixed charges cover 4.6; Net worth/fixed assets 82.4%; Net worth/total assets 61.8%
(*e*) *Investment*
Earnings per ordinary share 13p; Dividend cover for ordinary shares 1.3; Dividend yield 7.7%; Price/earnings ratio 10

15.6 £45 055

Answers to Numerical Questions 219

17.1		Year	Quantity	Price
		19-4	100	100
		19-5	117	120
		19-6	133	135
		19-7	158	155
		19-8	187	185
17.2	(ii)	19-6	100	
		19-7	112	
		19-8	121	
		19-9	138	
		19-0	151	

17.3	(iii)		Laspeyre	Paasche
		19-7	100	100
		19-8	110	110
		19-9	123	122

18.5 Current-cost loss £192 000
Current-cost balance sheet
— net assets and capital employed £4 800 000

18.6 Current-cost loss £495 000
Current-cost balance sheet
— net assets and capital employed £4 500 000

19.1 Cost of production £202 400; Gross profit £72 800; Net profit £10 100

19.2 (a) Marginal cost A £18 B £22
Profit A £4 800 B £9 600
(b) Profit A £10 800 B £19 800
(c) Product B

19.3 (a) (i) £270 (adverse) (ii) £400 (favourable)
(iii) £145 (favourable) (iv) £240 (adverse)

19.4 (a) Overdrafts: September £760
October £1 061
November £1 490
December £1 950
(b) Gross profit £5 000
Net profit £680
Fixed assets £7 840

		Current assets	£9 800
		Capital	£13 600
		Current liabilities	£4 040

19.5   (a)   Approximate quarterly sales — Quarter 1 £185 000; 2 £255 000; 3 £120 000; 4 £270 000

        (b)   Approximate salesmen's commissions   £34 000

               Approximate travelling and entertaining   £9 000

19.6   (a)   Increase in bank balance   £36 200

19.8

	19-5	19-6
Profitability		
Rate of gross profit	30%	31.7%
Rate of net profit	6%	8.3%
Return on capital employed	10.6%	15.3%
Liquidity		
Current ratio	2.25	3.0
Acid test ratio	1.4	1.4
Asset usage		
Debtor collection	36.5 days	42.6 days
Stock turnover	4.7	4.6
Sales/fixed assets	2.17	2.5
Capital structure		
Cover fixed charges	7	7.25
Net worth/total assets	68.3%	66.7%
Net worth/fixed assets	122%	125%
Investment		
Earnings ordinary share	7.5p	12.5p
Ordinary dividend cover	1.5	1.7
Dividend yield	11.1%	15%
Price/earnings ratio	7.3	8.3

19.9   Laspeyre index   328

        Base-year sales   £321 800

        Current-year sales at

           base-year prices   £295 731   (full year)

19.10   Current-cost loss   £78 000

         Current-cost balance sheet —

            assets and capital employed   £1 250 000